OUR WORLD OF SCIENCE

Science Every Day

By Gerald S. Craig
Professor of Natural Sciences
Teachers College, Columbia University

and Sara E. Baldwin
Department of Education
State Teachers College
West Chester, Pennsylvania

Illustrated by Janet Smalley,
Jeanne McLavy *and* Else Bostelmann

Ginn and Company

Boston · New York · Chicago · Atlanta · Dallas · Columbus
San Francisco · Toronto · London

C3

COPYRIGHT, 1950, BY GINN AND COMPANY
COPYRIGHT, 1946, BY GINN AND COMPANY
PHILIPPINES COPYRIGHT, 1950, BY GINN AND COMPANY

ALL RIGHTS RESERVED

550.7

OUR WORLD OF SCIENCE

Science All About Us
CRAIG · BURKE

Science through the Year
CRAIG · DANIEL

Science Every Day
CRAIG · BALDWIN

Exploring in Science
CRAIG · HURLEY

Working with Science
CRAIG · HILL

New Ideas in Science
CRAIG · HYDE

Going Forward with Science
CRAIG · LEWIS

Science Plans for Tomorrow
CRAIG · URBAN

The Athenæum Press
GINN AND COMPANY · PROPRIETORS · BOSTON · U.S.A.

Contents

	PAGE
Day Sky and Night Sky	4
How Some Animals Live and Grow	32
Many Ways to Live and Grow	78
Animal Homes	102
What a Magnet Can Do	134
The World Uses Electricity	144
We Live in Air	168
Water for You and Me	194
How Long Is a Lifetime?	218
Index	245

Day Sky and Night Sky

Morning

Morning has come to Your Town. The sun just shows itself above the hill.

Most boys and girls are asleep. Most mothers and fathers are asleep.

West   East

But the birds are awake. They are singing their morning songs.

The policeman is awake. He watched over the town all night.

The milkman is awake. He has started his day's work.

The sun is coming up in the east. It makes long shadows on the quiet street.

The policeman has on a warm coat. The milkman has buttoned his jacket to keep warm.

Soon Your Town will be awake.

School Time

Your Town is awake now. Trucks and wagons make the street a busy place.

It is time for people to go to their work. It is time for boys and girls to go to school.

The shadows are not so long as they were. Your Town is growing warmer. People have not buttoned their coats to keep warm. Children walk to school in the warm sunshine.

Where is the sun now?

Noon

Your Town is a busy town. Trucks and wagons go up and down the streets. People go in and out of stores. The clock strikes twelve. It is noon.

Many people are walking on the street. They walk along in the sunshine. They cannot walk in the shadows now. At noon shadows are very short.

Most of the people have taken off their coats. Noon is a warm time of day.

Where is the sun now?

West   East

After School

School time is over. Boys and girls have gone home from school. Playtime is here for children.

Look at the shadows on the street. Now there is more shadow than sunshine.

The children run and play and swing and jump. They are glad to have their coats and caps on. The day is growing much cooler.

Look at the sun. In what part of the sky do you see the sun now?

West   East

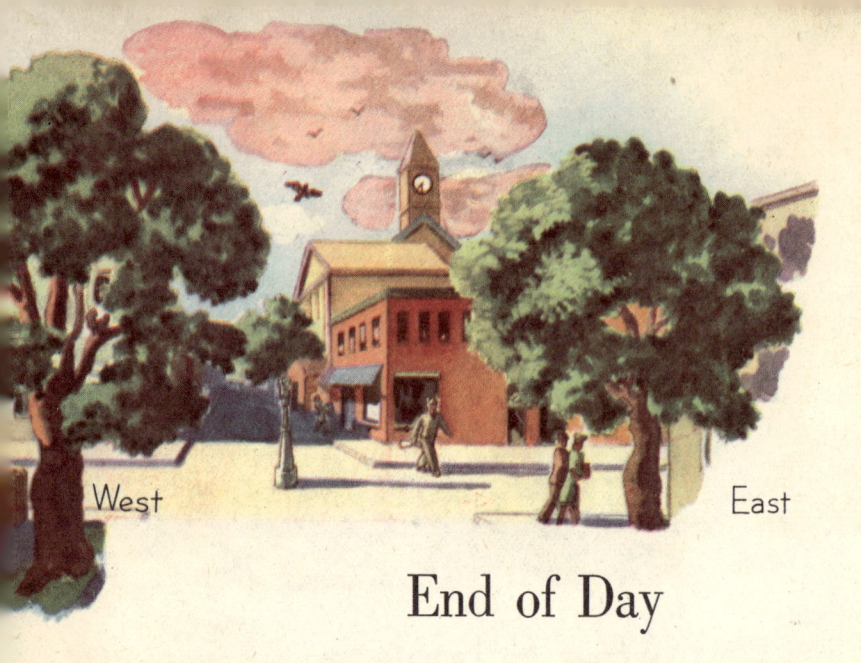

End of Day

Day is going away from Your Town.

Most people have stopped their work. Many children are in their beds.

A little noise comes from the trees. Birds are finding a place to rest. A gray squirrel jumps from limb to limb in the tree. Soon he will find a place to sleep.

Down in the long grass a rabbit goes hoppety, hoppety. Where will it sleep tonight?

The sun is going down in the west. Night is almost here.

Night

Night has come to Your Town.

It is dark and quiet now. Noisy, busy trucks and wagons have gone away.

Children are asleep. Most fathers and mothers are asleep. Chickens, rabbits, most of your pets are asleep.

But some animals are awake. A cat walks across the yard. A mouse runs about getting food. Some earthworms come up out of the ground. Down by the brook an old raccoon catches a fish for his supper.

Some people are awake, too. Policemen walk up and down the street. Engineers and conductors are busy on the trains. Some people work in factories at night.

Night is the time for most living things to rest. For others, it is the time to work.

Night is dark. People cannot see the sun. But they can see to find their way about.

The night sky has some light. Many, many, many stars shine down on the earth.

One star alone gives us very little light. Many stars together give enough light for us to see to walk about.

The moon gives us bright light. It gives us more light than all the stars in the sky.

The moon and the stars make the earth light at night. But they do not give us so much light as the sun does. Day always has more light than night has.

Night and day are as different as can be.

Sunlight and Shadows

The earth is light wherever the sun shines on it. It is dark where the sun does not shine.

The sun shines on Martha. It shines all around her body. But it cannot shine through her body.

There is a dark place on the ground by Martha. It is dark because the sun does not shine on that spot. This dark spot is Martha's shadow.

In the picture you see the sun. You see Martha and her shadow.

West   East

One sunny morning Martha went to the store for her mother. Her shadow was in front of her all the way.

When she walked home from the store, her shadow was behind her.

West   East

The next morning Martha went to school. Her shadow was in front of her. When she went home in the afternoon, her shadow was in front again. It did not follow behind her as it did when she walked home from the store.

"How does this happen?" Martha wondered. "My shadow followed behind me when I went home from the store. Why does it not follow behind me when I go home from school?"

Can you tell why Martha's shadow did not follow her home from school?

Look at the picture of Your Town on page 7. It is school time in the morning. The sun comes up in the east. The shadows fall to the west when the sun is coming up.

Look at the picture on page 9. It is after school in the afternoon. The sun goes down in the west. The shadows fall to the east when the sun is going down.

When Martha went to school in the morning, the sun was in the east. The sun was behind her. Her shadow was in front of her.

When she went home from school in the afternoon, the sun was in the west. The sun was behind her again. So her shadow was in front of her and not behind her as she went home from school.

The Changing Moon

Mary is happy. Grandmother is coming for a visit. She is coming just in time for supper.

Father, Mother, and Mary are at the train to meet her. On the way home they see the moon in the sky.

Where is the moon in the picture? You can see just a small part of the moon tonight. But it gives a bright light.

It is just a week since Grandmother came to visit. It is Mary's birthday. Bill and Martha have had supper at Mary's house.

They are going home in the bright moonlight. The big round moon is starting to shine above the hill.

Look at the moon in the picture. Does it look as it did when Grandmother came?

Now the moon gives the earth much light Look at the children's shadows in the bright moonlight.

Almost two weeks have gone by since Grandmother came. It is twelve o'clock at night. Jip is barking. Mother and Father and Mary have waked up. Father has gone out to see why Jip is barking.

Mary is looking out of the window. The moon has come up behind the hill. It is the same moon she watched on her birthday, but tonight she can see just a part of it.

Soon Father comes back into the house.

" Some animal tried to get our chickens," he says. " But Jip scared it away. We must go back to sleep now."

The moon shines on in the sky. Does it look as it did when Grandmother came?

One more week has gone by. It is Mary's bedtime. The clock strikes eight.

Mary always looks out of the window before she goes to bed. She likes to look at the night sky.

"You will not see the moon tonight," her mother says. "This is the dark of the moon. There will be no moonlight all night.

"Look for the moon tomorrow night," her mother tells her. "Then you will see a little part of the moon. You will see the new moon."

Still another week has gone by. It is just four weeks since Grandmother came to Mary's house. She has been there about a month. Tonight she is going home.

Mother, Father, and Mary have come to the train with Grandmother. It is almost supper time. Grandmother will have supper on the train. She will sleep on the train.

A little moon is in the sky. It looks the way it did when Grandmother came.

In four more weeks, the moon will look the same way again. The moon makes the same changes every month.

The moon looks a little different each week.

In the first week it looks as it did when Mary's grandmother came to visit. We can see just a small part of the moon. Just a small part of the moon gives us light. This is called the moon's first quarter.

The second week the moon looks big and round. This is the way it looked on Mary's birthday. This is the second quarter. It is called the full moon.

The third week just a part of the moon gives us light. The moon looked this way when Jip waked up Mary's family. This is the moon's third, or last quarter.

In the fourth week we have the dark of the moon. For one night no light comes to us from the moon.

Just a month has gone by since the beginning of the first week. Now we see a very little light at the other edge of the moon. This is called the new moon. Can you tell why?

23

What Is the Moon Like?

Mary wondered and wondered about the moon. She watched it each night.

"If I should stand on a mountain, could I reach the moon?" she asked.

"No," said her father. "You would not be high enough to reach the moon."

"Can an airplane reach the moon?" Mary wanted to know.

"Oh, no," her father answered. "An airplane cannot fly to the moon. The moon is far, far out in the sky. No one ever has gone to the moon."

Suppose that you and Mary could go to the moon. Do you know what you would find out there in the sky?

You would not find just a big, bright light. The moon is not like a giant street light.

You would find a place that is like our earth in some ways. There would be ground to walk upon. There are high mountains and big flat places. There are many, many rocks.

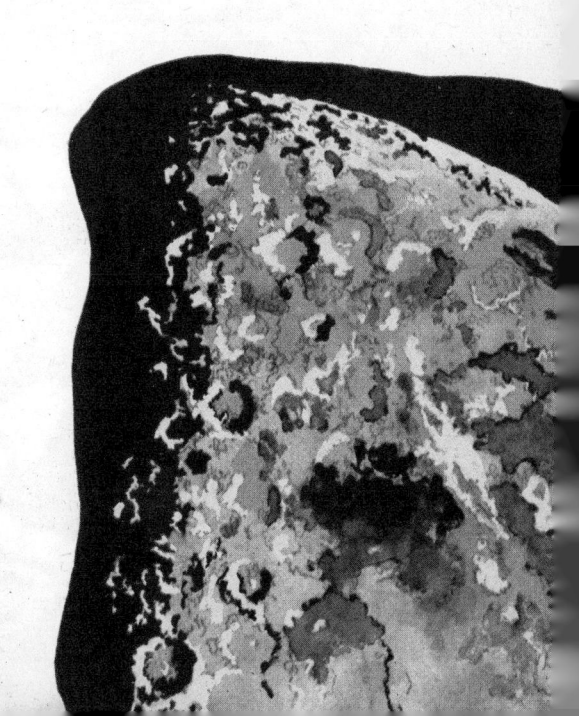

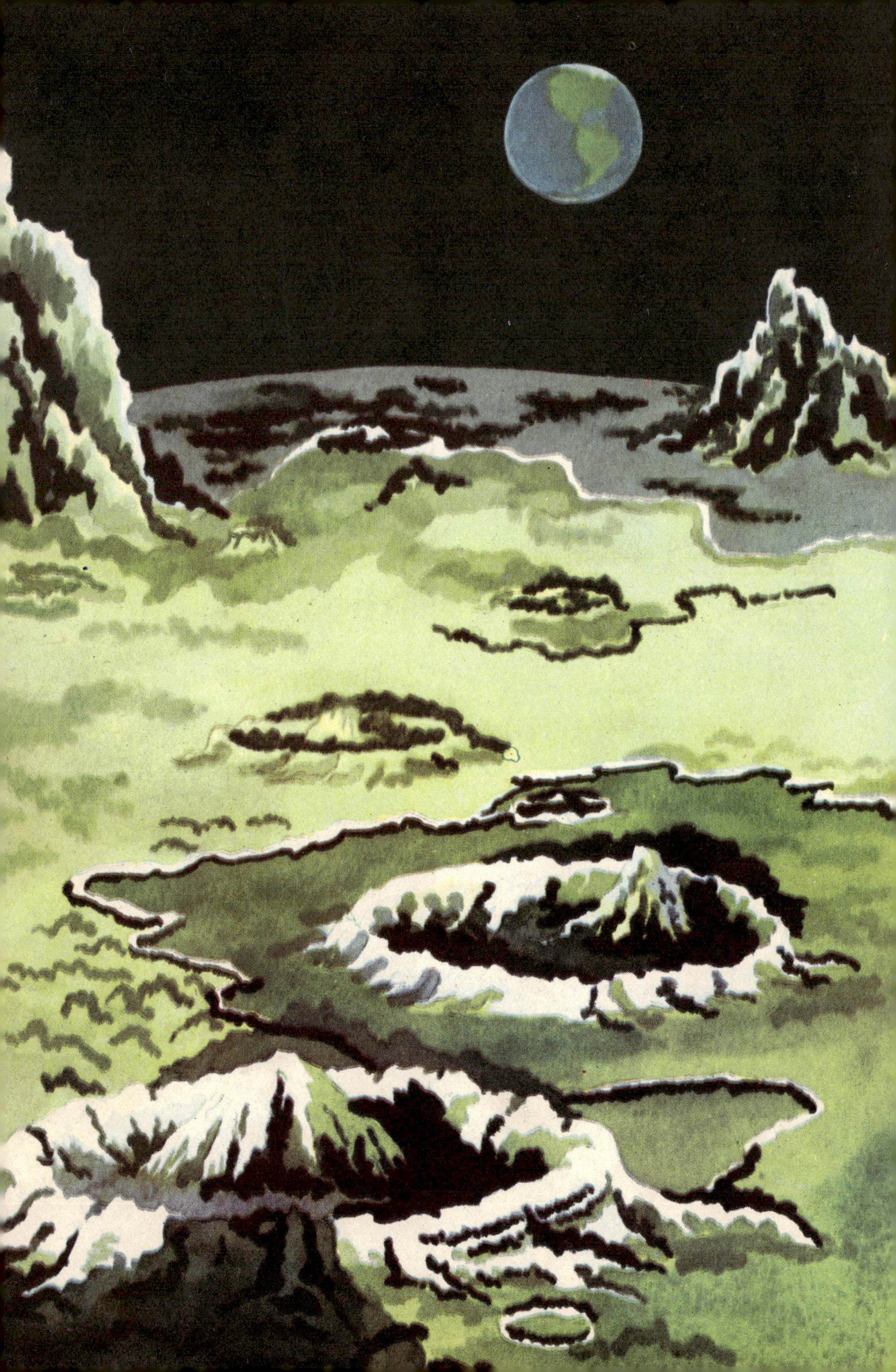

But you would not think you were on the earth. The moon is very different. You would not see grass and trees. You would see just rocks.

Wherever you looked, you would see rocks, rocks, and more rocks. Rocks would be all around you on the big, round moon!

You could not climb the mountains of the moon. The mountains of the moon are made of rock. The sides go straight up from the ground.

Suppose you tried to climb over some rocky places near the ground. Soon you would say, " Oh, my poor feet ! "

The rocks on the moon are sharp and pointed. They would cut your feet.

Suppose you wanted a drink of water. If you should travel all over the moon, you could not get a drink of water. The moon does not have water.

You would find no wells or springs on the moon. There are no ponds or lakes or rivers.

"Oh, I'll get some water when it rains," you would say.

Then you would look for clouds in the sky. But no clouds would be floating above you. There are no clouds on the moon. Rain never falls there.

You could not get a drink of water anywhere on the moon.

"Then I'll take a drink of milk," you would say.

No, you could not take a drink of milk. Cows do not live on the moon. Grass does not grow on the moon. There is no water to make grass grow. There is no water for cows to drink. Nothing grows on the moon as it does on the earth.

You would just have to wait for your drink until you got back to earth.

There would be one good thing about this trip to the moon. Your hat would not blow off. The wind does not blow, out there on the moon.

You would not see leaves blowing about in the wind. There are no leaves on the moon. There are no trees. There is no wind.

You would not see birds or butterflies flying about in the air. There is no air for them to fly in.

"Oh, my!" you would say. "There is no air for birds here. There is no air for butterflies. There is no air for cows. There is no air for me."

That is right. There is no air to breathe on the moon.

So you would come back to the good old earth to find air to breathe. You would come back the same way you went — just supposing!

Make a Moon Book

1. Watch the moon on the same night of the week for four weeks. Make a picture of the way the moon looks on each night. Be careful to make the first quarter and the last quarter right.

2. Suppose you could take a trip to the moon. Make a picture of the way you think the moon would look.

3. Tell a story about some things that could not happen on the moon.

Look to Find Out

You know that the sun makes shadows. Other lights, too, make shadows.

Look for shadows in the moonlight at the time of the full moon.

Look around a room at night. Look at shadows that are made by the lights in your home.

A Paper Shadow

These children are making a shadow out of paper. They will put the paper shadow upon the wall of the schoolroom.

Try this on a sunny day. Cut out one shadow as soon as you reach school in the morning. Cut out another shadow at noon.

Which shadow will be longer? Can you tell why?

How Some Animals Live and Grow

A Box Turtle's Nest

It was a sunny autumn day. Bright leaves blew about in the wind. Birds flew through the air on their way to the south.

Bob and Bill were walking through the fields. They liked to walk and look, and look and walk. They liked to find out what was happening out of doors.

"Oh, see!" said Bill. "Something is coming out of the ground."

"Where?" asked Bob.

"Right under that yellow leaf by the fence," said Bill.

The boys watched the place by the fence. A small turtle crawled out of the ground. It was not much bigger than a penny.

"Well, I never!" said Bob. "That looks like a new baby turtle."

"It walks so funny," said Bill.

"I think it is just learning how to walk," said Bob.

Soon another little turtle tried to come out of the ground. It worked and it worked. Then it, too, was out of the ground.

The boys watched. Four more baby turtles worked their way out of the ground.

The little turtles walked away through the grass.

The boys did not touch the turtles or take them in their hands. They watched very quietly. They did not make the turtles afraid.

Each baby turtle crawled away under the leaves by the fence.

"Those turtles have just come out of the eggs," said Bill. "Who would ever know a turtle's nest was there?"

The mother turtle had spread earth over her nest. Some sticks and leaves were spread over the nest, too. Most of you would not know a nest was there.

One warm, summer day Mother Turtle had laid the eggs. She had spread earth and leaves over the nest. Then she had crawled away.

She did not come back to the nest. She did not watch the eggs. She would not need to take care of the baby turtles.

The eggs had stayed in the ground for three months. Then baby turtles had crawled out of the eggs. On that very day, Bob and Bill had found the nest.

A Box Turtle's Shell

The body of a turtle has a covering called a shell. A box turtle has a very fine shell. It is brown with yellow spots, and it is hard like bone.

The underside of the shell has two parts. The turtle can make these parts go up and down. They can drop open something like doors.

When these parts are open, the turtle's head comes out of the shell. Its legs and tail come out of the shell, too.

When the turtle is afraid, it pulls its head, legs, and tail into its shell.

It pulls up the doors to the under part. All of its body is in the shell. The shell is like a box around the turtle's body. It is as hard as bone. You cannot open it.

A turtle's head, legs, and tail would make good food for some animals. But a box turtle pulls these into its shell very quickly when danger is near.

A box turtle's shell does not make good eating. So most animals leave box turtles alone. They are safe from animal enemies.

What Box Turtles Eat

Some turtles live in water, but a box turtle is not a water turtle. It is a land turtle. It lives on the ground and travels about in the woods and fields.

A box turtle finds many different kinds of food to eat. Much of its food is plant food. It eats many kinds of berries that grow in the fields and woods.

A box turtle eats many, many insects. It eats earthworms and snails.

Box Turtles in Winter

The fall days were growing cold when Bill and Bob found the baby turtles. The boys looked and looked for the turtles, but they never saw them again. Bill wondered how they could live through the cold winter days.

The little turtles ate and ate. They grew bigger and bigger.

At last when the days were very, very cold the turtles stopped looking for food. They wiggled their way into the ground. Down, down, down they wiggled. They were away from the freezing cold.

"How can they eat down there in the ground?" Bob wondered.

"They do not eat," his father told him. "They do not eat all winter long."

"Don't they get very, very hungry?" Bill asked.

"Not in the winter time," his father said. "The turtles are resting then. They do not need to eat anything when they are resting. They have food stored away in their bodies."

The Little Turtles Grow Up

At last spring came. The days grew warmer. The ground grew warmer. The turtles came out of the ground and looked for food. They ate and ate.

All summer they stayed in the grass and under the leaves. When winter came again, they wiggled into the ground.

Each year the turtles were a little bigger than they were the year before. When they were about five years old, they were grown-up turtles.

Then they did not need to hide away in the grass and leaves. They walked about in places where people could see them.

Box turtles are a help to people. They eat many of the insects that eat plants in your garden. They eat snails, house flies, and mosquitoes.

Try to find a box turtle when you are out of doors. Look for it in the fields and along the road or in your yard.

If you ever find a box turtle, will you take good care of it? Will you watch it quietly without touching it? Will you try to help it to live on for many, many years?

A Caterpillar Meets a Butterfly

A big caterpillar was eating a leaf of a milkweed plant.

It was a beautiful caterpillar. It had a yellow head. On its head were two black stripes.

Colored stripes went round and round its body. It had yellow stripes and stripes of black and white.

A bright-colored butterfly was flying near by. It stopped to taste the sweet flower of the milkweed plant.

It was a beautiful butterfly. Its wings were a dark orange color. The edges of the wings were black with white and yellow spots.

There are many, many different kinds of butterflies in the world. This was a monarch butterfly.

The caterpillar crawled slowly about on the leaf. The butterfly flew quickly away.

The caterpillar did not look at the butterfly. The butterfly did not look at the caterpillar.

The butterfly did not know that once it was a caterpillar like the one on the leaf. The caterpillar did not know that soon it would be a butterfly like the one on the milkweed flower.

The Life of a Monarch Butterfly

Tiny green balls were on the underside of the milkweed leaves. The tiny green balls were eggs. A butterfly had laid these eggs a short time before.

Try to find the eggs of the monarch butterfly. You can see them in the spring, in the summer, or in the fall. You should always look for them on the leaves of the milkweed plant.

The eggs are very small. They are green like the leaf. If the eggs could grow big, they would look like this.

Soon a little caterpillar comes out of each egg. It is called a larva. It eats the leaves of the milkweed plant.

The larva eats and grows, eats and grows. At first it is not much of any color. Then it grows to be black and white. By and by it is a big, bright-colored caterpillar.

At this time a queer thing happens to the caterpillar. It fastens one end of its body to a leaf. It hangs from the leaf with its head down.

Little by little the old covering of its body comes off. Little by little it gets a new covering. The new covering is like a bag. It is soft and green. At the top and at the bottom are spots that look like gold. Now the caterpillar is called a pupa.

Soon the covering grows hard. The bag hangs from the leaf for about two weeks. Some people say, " Now the caterpillar is resting in its green bag." But much is happening to the body of the caterpillar at this time.

In about two weeks the green covering breaks open. Do you think a caterpillar comes out of the bag? No. Out comes a bright-colored monarch butterfly.

At first it is not very pretty. Its wings were folded over and over when it was in the green bag. But the butterfly slowly spreads them out until they are big and strong. Then it flies away.

Monarch Butterflies in Winter

What does a monarch butterfly do when cold weather comes? It cannot fly about in the freezing winds of winter.

Many kinds of butterflies live as pupae through the cold weeks of winter. Their hard covering saves them from freezing.

But monarch butterflies keep away from winter cold in a different way. When fall days grow cold, monarch butterflies start on a long trip.

First they fly to a tree in the woods or field. Hundreds of them come together in one tree. Others fly to trees that are near by. Hundreds of monarch butterflies start to fly south together.

At last the butterflies come to a place where it is warm. They stop flying and rest in trees. All winter they rest in the trees. On warm, sunny days they fly away on short trips. They take a little food from flowers and then they fly back to the trees.

Monarch Butterflies in Summer

When spring comes, monarch butterflies start to fly north. Many butterflies stop to lay eggs on milkweed plants.

Some larvae come out of the eggs. They grow into larger caterpillars and these caterpillars grow into pupae. Soon the pupae are bright colored butterflies.

These butterflies, too, fly on north. They, too, stop to lay eggs. Then the story takes place all over again.

Monarch Butterflies Are Not Afraid

Monarch butterflies do not have many enemies because they have a bad taste. Most birds and other insects do not like to eat them.

It is fun to watch monarch butterflies flying about. They are not afraid of birds. Sometimes they fly about with them.

They are not so afraid of people as most butterflies are. You can make a butterfly come to you.

Take a flower in your hand and stand very quietly in your garden. If monarch butterflies are in the garden, one of them may fly to you. Sometimes one will sit on your hand.

Here Come the Sunfish!

Peter and Polly were watching quietly. They were looking into the water of a brook on their farm. They were looking for sunfish.

The water was clear and bright. Soon the fish flashed by in the sunlight.

Peter said, "Sunfish is a good name for these fish. They are bright like sunlight."

Sunfish are orange. They are shiny like gold. On each side of the head is a spot of black. Near the black spot is a bright stripe of red.

Polly said, "Sunfish are beautiful. I like their bright colors."

A sunfish is covered with scales. The scales make it look shiny like gold. The scales make a good covering. They keep the fish from getting scratched if something strikes it in the water.

How Fish Live in Water

Polly watched the sunfish swim about in the clear water. She wished that she could swim as well as they do.

Polly can swim very well, but she cannot swim under water as a fish can. She has to come up to the top of the water to get air to breathe.

People cannot live in water. Most animals cannot live in water. They cannot breathe when they are under water.

A fish lives in water. It takes in air under water. It gets its food in water. Water is its home.

Watch a fish as it takes in air under the water. Watch it open its mouth again and again.

You may ask, "Is the fish drinking?" No, it is not drinking the water. It is getting air that is in the water.

The water goes into the mouth of the fish. It goes out through the gills. Its gills help the fish to take in air that is in water.

In the picture of the sunfish, look at the black spot on the side of the head. This spot is on the cover of the gills of the sunfish. The next time you see a fish, look for its gills.

Enemies of Sunfish

Who do you think are some of the enemies of sunfish? Many water birds eat sunfish before they are grown up. Some water insects eat the young fish, too.

Boys and men like to catch sunfish. Sunfish are easy to catch. They are small but they are very good to eat.

Many, many sunfish live on, in the waters. Most people try to catch fish that are bigger than sunfish. So there will be enough sunfish, if people are careful not to take too many.

How Young Sunfish Grow Up

In the spring a mother sunfish lays many eggs. These eggs are laid in a nest. The nest is only a hole in the bottom of the brook. The sunfish makes the hole with its tail. It is a good place for sunfish eggs.

When the mother fish has laid the eggs, the father fish drives her away. If she stays, she will eat the eggs.

The father fish watches the eggs. Water birds and water insects eat the eggs of many fish. But they do not eat so many of the eggs of sunfish. The father sunfish takes good care of the eggs.

By and by young fish come out of the eggs. Then the father swims away.

The young fish are very small when they wiggle out of the eggs. But they look very much like the grown-up fish.

The little fish can swim as soon as they are out of the eggs. They can find food. They do not need a mother's care.

Many, many young sunfish do not live to grow up. Other fish like to eat them. Other water animals eat them too.

But many young sunfish do live to grow up. Their scales are not so shiny and bright as those of the grown-up fish. Many of them swim away before their enemies see them.

Sunfish in Winter Time

Do you wonder what saves sunfish from freezing in winter?

Some animals go away from winter's cold. They go to a warm place for the winter. But sunfish do not go away. They do not leave their homes.

Some animals crawl into the ground in winter. But sunfish do not go into the ground.

Sometimes ice covers the water where they live. But the sunfish stay in the water. Water near the bottom does not freeze. The sunfish stay near the bottom of the brooks under the ice.

They do not race through the water as they do in summer. In the winter time they are quiet. But spring always comes. Then the bright sunfish swim together again through the clear water.

Look for the Song Sparrow

If you live in the country, you have seen song sparrows. If you live in the city, you may have seen them, too. They live in the east and in the west. They live in the north and in the south.

Some song sparrows live in mountains. Others are found in lowlands. Many live in fields and woods where there is water. Others live in places that are very dry.

There are many kinds of song sparrows.

Song sparrow is a good name for this little brown bird. Most of the year you can hear his song.

Before winter's snow has gone away, song sparrows begin to come back from the south. They start to sing as soon as they are here.

A cold winter wind is blowing through the trees. A song sparrow sits on a limb with his feathers puffed out around him.

"Che-enk, ch-enk!" The song sparrow's voice tells you that spring is on the way.

His first songs are not very pretty. He just goes, "Chenk, ch-enk, chenk!" But that is better than no song at all.

Song sparrows can live very well in the cold days before spring. They know where to look for food.

Many weeds grow along the side of the road and in the fields. Song sparrows find the weeds and eat the seeds.

The birds help farmers when they eat these seeds. Farmers do not like to have weeds on their farms. The seeds that are eaten by sparrows do not grow into more weeds.

A Song Sparrow's Nest

When spring comes, song sparrows are very busy. Does anyone need to tell you what keeps them busy? Like most other birds, they are busy making nests. They are busy taking care of their baby birds.

All through the spring, their song is very beautiful. They sing and sing and sing.

Most song sparrows make their nests in bushes. If you ever try to find a song sparrow's nest, look in places that are near the ground.

A song sparrow's nest is not very pretty. For the outside, the birds use dry grass and old leaves. Sometimes they put in small pieces of bark. Sometimes they use small sticks.

The inside of the nest is made with more care. Hair and small grasses are placed around and around the inside. This makes a soft, warm place for the baby birds.

A mother song sparrow lays about four eggs. You would like to look at these eggs. Some are light blue. Some are light green. They look as if someone had painted little brown spots all over them.

Young Song Sparrows

In about two weeks young birds come out of the eggs. They are not pretty little birds. They have no feathers. Their eyes are not open. They cannot walk or fly. They can just stay in the nest and cry for something to eat.

Then the mother bird is very busy. The father bird helps her. They fly away from the nest to get food for the hungry little ones. Then they fly back again. Away for more food and back to the nest! All day long, the mother and father are busy.

The song sparrows find caterpillars for the baby birds. They find many other insects that eat plants and trees. They eat some of these insects themselves. At nesting time song sparrows are a great help to farmers. Can you tell why?

In about a week, the eyes of the little birds are open. They have some feathers but they cannot fly. For another week the mother brings food to the young birds.

By and by the young birds can fly a little. They take many short trips from the nest and back again. At last they can fly about without any help. They go far away from the nest and do not come back. They do not need a mother to watch over them now.

What do you think the mother bird does then? Do you think she takes a long rest after her hard work?

No, she does not take a rest. She lays some more eggs. Soon more baby birds are crying for something to eat.

For another two weeks mother song sparrow hurries again. She hurries from the nest for food. She hurries back to her hungry babies.

At last these young birds are ready to leave the nest. Does the mother bird take a rest now? No, she soon lays more eggs. In a short time she is flying about to find food for more baby birds.

By the end of summer, song sparrows are ready for a rest. For a time you do not see song sparrows hopping around. You do not hear their bright, happy song. They are hiding away in the bushes.

When autumn days come, song sparrows are flying about again. They are fine-looking birds now. When they were hiding away, they lost their old feathers. They came back with fine new coats.

Watching for Enemies

All through the year song sparrows must watch out for their enemies. They must watch out for cats.

Song sparrows must watch out for other birds. Hawks and owls like to eat them. They must watch out for squirrels too. These animals take the eggs from the nest.

What helps to save a song sparrow from his enemies?

A song sparrow can see very well. With his bright eyes he sees an enemy as it comes near. He can move very fast, too. He can fly away quickly from a cat or a squirrel.

He has to move very quickly to get away from a hawk or an owl. A song sparrow always is watching. He always is ready to fly away quickly.

Song Sparrows in Winter

All through the fall many birds are leaving their summer homes. Bluebirds, robins, wrens, yellow warblers, swallows, ducks — all fly south to winter homes.

But song sparrows are not ready to fly away. They spend the fall in the homes where they lived all summer. They scratch in the leaves. They look for insects. They eat the seeds of many weeds. They have fine, warm coats of feathers. They live very well in the cold fall days.

At last the snow comes. Cold winds blow the song sparrows about. Then they, too, start for a warm home to the south.

They stay there for a short time. Then back they come. Again you hear their songs that tell you spring is on the way.

Cougars at Home

It was the end of day. The sun was going down. Mother cougar and her four kittens waited for father cougar. Soon he would come to them with food.

Mother cougar and the kittens lay on the floor of their home. It was a good home. It was away from rain and cold winds. It was away from most enemies of cougars.

This cougar family had made their home on the side of a mountain. It was in a place where great rocks made a floor and a roof. It was a cave among the rocks. The cave was like a small room under the ground.

At the front of the cave was a hole. This hole was just big enough to be used as a door. The cougars went in and out of the cave through this hole.

Mother cougar lay near the hole. She was watching for father cougar. Soon her ears moved a little. She knew that father cougar was near.

Then she saw him standing in the doorway. In his mouth was a young goat. The cougars would have a dinner of goat that night.

A cougar is a beautiful animal. Its color is light brown. It has a fine-looking coat of fur.

A cougar has a big strong body. It is about five feet long. Its tail is long and heavy.

The cougar's legs are strong. Its paws are big, and its claws are long and sharp.

A cougar has a big head. Its mouth is not very big, but the teeth are sharp and strong.

How Cougars Get Their Food

Your ears could not have heard father cougar coming up to the door of the cave. He moved quietly among the rocks. His feet made almost no noise as he walked.

This is one way cougars use to get their food. They move slowly and quietly until they are near the animal they want. Then they give a quick jump. They jump so quickly that the animal has no time to get away.

Sometimes a cougar lies flat on the limb of a tree. He lies there until an animal walks under the tree. Then with a quick strong jump he drops down upon it and one more animal is food for his family. Not many animals can get away from a cougar when he tries this trick. All animals try to keep out of the way of the cougar's strong claws.

The cougar is not friendly to any other animals. In all the woods and fields, no other animals are friendly to him.

The cougar can have almost any animal he wants for food. Sometimes he catches small animals. They are good eating for the cougar kittens. Rabbits, lambs, and birds of many kinds are eaten by cougar kittens.

But grown-up cougars can catch almost any animal they happen to meet. They sometimes catch young colts, sheep, and calves. They catch young deer and grown-up deer. They even take cows and grown-up horses for their dinner.

Sometimes cougars cannot find food near by. Then they travel about until they find something to eat. Sometimes the cougars travel miles and miles for food. Farmers watch their sheep and calves and colts when cougars are about.

Cougars rest in the daytime and go out for food at night. They look for food when many other animals are resting. Catching animals at rest is easy work for cougars.

The Care of Young Cougars

Cougars take good care of their young. They find a good home for them. They watch over them and bring food to them.

Sometimes the mother has two kittens. Sometimes she has three or four. The mother feeds them milk as a mother cat feeds her kittens.

For a time the mother stays with the kittens. The father brings food to her. When the kittens can have meat, he brings home small animals for them to eat. Soon the mother, too, goes out for food. The kittens stay by themselves.

When the kittens are old enough, they go out with the mother and father to find food. The mother and father show them how to get their own food.

Where Cougars Live

Cougars live in the North and in the South, in the East and in the West.

They make their homes in all kinds of places. Some cougars live in the woods. Others live in the open fields. Some make their homes on the sides of mountains. The cougars in the first part of this story had a fine home in a cave.

Some cougars make their homes out in the open. Some use a flat rock which has another rock above to keep out the rain. Others use a grassy place under some bushes.

Some cougars hide their home under trees which have branches near to the ground. It is not easy to find the home of a cougar.

Today there are not many cougars in places where people live. Most cougars now keep far back in the woods. They hide away high in the mountains.

Most of us do not want to meet cougars in the places where they live, but we can see them in cages at the park.

Something to Think About

There are many kinds of animals in the world. Some are a great help to people. Others are not.

Some animals take very good care of their babies. Others do not take care of their young at all.

Animals live in all kinds of places. They have many ways of getting food. They have many ways of moving about. They have many ways of getting away from their enemies. There are many ways for animals to live and grow.

Something to Try

Take a walk out of doors. Look about you. Find some animal to call your pet.

You may find a squirrel or a rabbit, some ants or some grasshoppers. You may find some eggs in a bird's nest. Watch for these, too.

Do not touch your new pet. Do not take it home with you. This is your out-of-door pet.

Every day go to the place where you first saw your pet. Watch to see what happens to it.

Watch to see how the pet eats. Watch to find out about its young. Try to find out what animals are its enemies. How does it get away from its enemies?

Watch to see how its body looks.

If you do this, you will learn many things about the out-of-doors.

Many Ways to Live and Grow

Tree where yellow warblers nest

Grassy places where skunks look for grasshoppers and beetles

Log at edge of water where frogs and turtles sun themselves

Place where cardinals nest

Brook where fish swim

Tree where squirrels and woodpeckers have holes

Stonewall under which snakes and chipmunks hide

Grassy places where horses and cows feed

Suppose you were a wild animal that lives in the woods or fields. It would keep you busy to stay alive.

First of all you would need to find food. Would you know where to look?

You would need to get away from cold and stormy weather.

You would need to stay out of the way of your animal enemies.

Do you think you could do all of these things for yourself?

Woodchuck's home in tunnel underground

Animals Must Have Food

There are many kinds of animals in the world. They eat many kinds of food.

Some animals eat only plants. Water animals eat water plants.

Is there a fish bowl in your schoolroom? Are there snails in it? Watch the snails as they move about. Have you seen them eating the water plants? Sometimes they are on the sides of the bowl, eating tiny green plants that grow there.

Land animals eat land plants. Rabbits sometimes eat plants in a garden. They eat grass and leaves. Woodchucks eat grass, grain, and vegetables.

Many other animals eat plants for food. Squirrels eat nuts. Deer eat leaves and branches of young trees.

The leaves of trees are often eaten away by caterpillars. In some places all of the farmers' crops have been eaten by grasshoppers. Farmers work hard to keep beetles and other insects from eating their grain, fruit, and vegetables.

Some animals do not use plants for food. They eat other animals. We call these meat-eating animals.

You know now that cougars catch animals for food. Wildcats eat many kinds of small animals. Lions and tigers are meat-eating animals, too.

Eagle   Sparrow hawk   Owl

Some birds, too, are meat eaters. Owls and hawks sometimes eat chickens and other birds. But they do much good by eating mice, grasshoppers, and beetles. Hawks and eagles catch fish. Eagles eat other birds and rabbits, and they will even carry away small lambs.

Some animals eat many kinds of food. Catbirds, chickadees, blue jays and other birds eat insects of almost all kinds that are found near by. Many birds eat seeds of weeds. They eat fruit of all kinds.

Robin   Oriole   Chickadee

Some animals go on living because they can eat almost anything they find.

Black bears eat many kinds of small animals. They eat ants, fish, frogs, mice, and birds. Bears like plant food. Corn, nuts, or berries make a good dinner. They like honey too.

Mice and rats eat almost any food. They eat any food that people eat. They eat grain, fruit, and chickens. They even eat books and papers. They eat their way through wood. Not all these things are good food for mice and rats. But they eat them just the same.

Some animals always eat about the same kind of food. Beavers eat the bark of trees. Caterpillars of the monarch butterfly always feed on milkweed plants. Horses and cows eat grass or hay and grain. Day after day these animals eat the same kinds of food.

Some animals eat very, very tiny plants or animals. Most of the food of tadpoles is so small that we cannot see it in the water.

Many insects eat other insects smaller than themselves. Spiders eat flies. A beetle called a ladybird eats hundreds of tiny insects that live on plants.

Chickadees, song sparrows, wrens, and many other birds eat small seeds of weeds.

Some animals eat other large animals. Mountain lions or wolves can catch young colts or calves or deer for food. Hungry lions will eat a zebra.

There are many kinds of animals in the world. They eat many kinds of food.

Many Ways to Catch Food

Animals which eat other animals must be fast workers. No animal wants to be the food of another animal.

A cat wants a mouse or a bird for its dinner. How does it get it? Quietly and watchfully it moves along. Then a quick jump and the cat has food!

A frog sits very still in the sun. It is waiting for an insect to come by. Soon a mosquito comes buzzing along. A quick flip, out goes the frog's tongue, and the mosquito is inside the frog.

Lions, tigers, and cougars are quick hard fighters. Each one can bring home for food an animal much larger than itself. All these animals have long, sharp claws. They can scratch deep. Their teeth are long and sharp. They can bite even through bones.

A tiger sees a cow which it wants for food. The cow is a bigger animal than the tiger. But the cow will be food for the tiger. Quietly and watchfully the tiger moves. A quick jump! The sharp claws scratch. The sharp teeth bite. The tiger has a cow for dinner.

A wolf is a strong animal. It can catch sheep and calves and young colts. But wolves have another way to get an animal for food. Many wolves go together to catch their food. Together they are very strong.

The deer is a big animal. It can run fast. But it is not easy for it to get away from the hungry wolves which run together.

In Stormy Weather

Suppose again that you were a wild animal of the woods or fields. Could you keep warm in cold times and stormy weather?

In cold or stormy times you wear warm coats, caps, and leggings. Animals with fur or feathers need warmer covering when cold times come along.

In autumn many animals start to get new coats. The summer coat of fur or feathers is not warm enough for winter. This coat starts to come off.

You have seen the hair that comes out of your dog's coat. It comes off on chairs and on people's suits or dresses. Your dog's summer coat is coming off.

A warmer winter coat starts to take its place. By the time cold weather comes, your dog's new winter coat is all grown out. Many animals get new coats in this same way.

For many animals the new winter coat is not the same color as the summer coat.

The summer coats of rabbits are brown. The winter coat is more nearly gray. Some kinds of rabbits have white coats in winter. The gray squirrel's winter coat is a real gray. Its summer coat has much brown in it.

The brown chickadee has a gray and black coat in winter.

You go into your house to get away from cold and storms. Where could you go if you lived in the fields or woods?

Would you look for trees and bushes growing close together? Blue jays and some other birds go into evergreen trees. Leaves of evergreen trees are called needles. The needles of the evergreen trees fall in close and thick around them. They keep away cold winds and snow.

Some birds and other small animals crawl under low piles of cornstalks, bushes, or thick grasses. Snow may fall over the grasses, cornstalks, and bushes. But the animals are away from the cold wind.

Some animals look for a hole in the ground. Rabbits sometimes crawl into a woodchuck's hole. Sometimes they find a hole under a tree.

Skunks find holes in the ground. A raccoon climbs into the trunk of an old tree to keep warm. Squirrels find holes in the trees.

Some animals get ready for winter before the cold days come.

Woodchucks dig long holes under the ground. They go into these homes in the fall. Then they curl themselves up and take a long rest.

They stay in their holes all winter. Only the warm days of spring will bring them out of the ground.

Chipmunks, too, dig holes in the ground in the fall. They curl up and rest in the cold days of winter. Frogs, toads, and turtles go into the mud.

Bears, raccoons, and skunks take a long rest in the winter time. On warm days they come out for food. Then they go back into their resting places to sleep.

Muskrats and beavers build fine houses in the water. In the winter they sleep much of the time in their warm homes.

Some animals do not need to do any of these things in winter. They go away from the cold and snow.

In autumn the sky is full of birds. You have seen them flying together over the tops of houses and trees.

Away they go to the south — robins, bluebirds, swallows, wrens, warblers, and wild ducks.

Every autumn hundreds, hundreds, and hundreds of birds fly to the warm lands to the south. There they find food. There they are safe from cold winds and snowstorms.

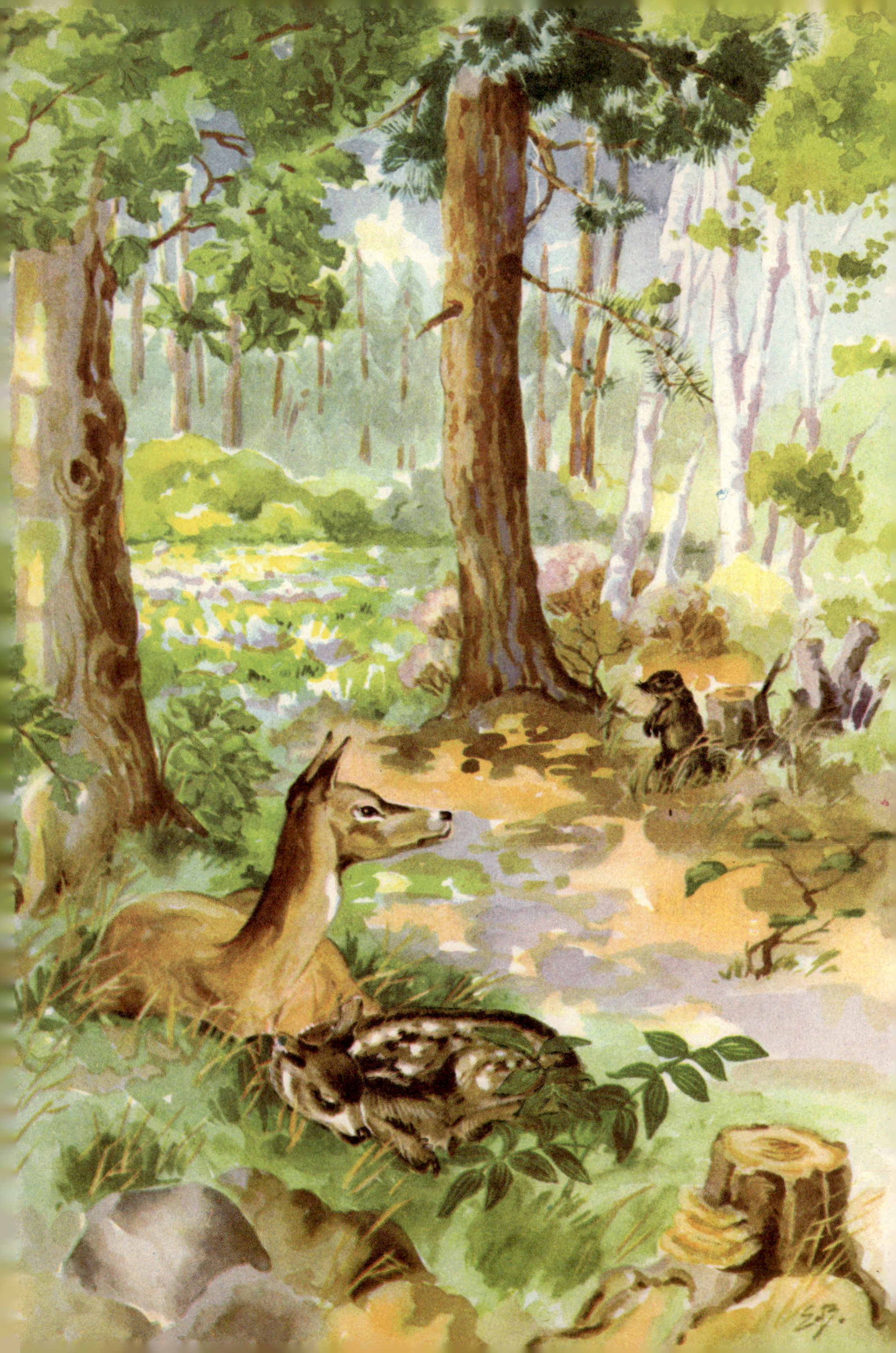

Animals and Their Enemies

Suppose you had a fine little spotted baby deer. Would you know how to keep it safe? The mother deer knows. Both the mother and her baby stay very still on their bed of leaves in the woods. They look much like their home, and enemies do not see them easily.

How many animals can you find in the picture? Could you find all of them right away?

Their color is much like the color of the place where they stay. Their color hides them from their enemies.

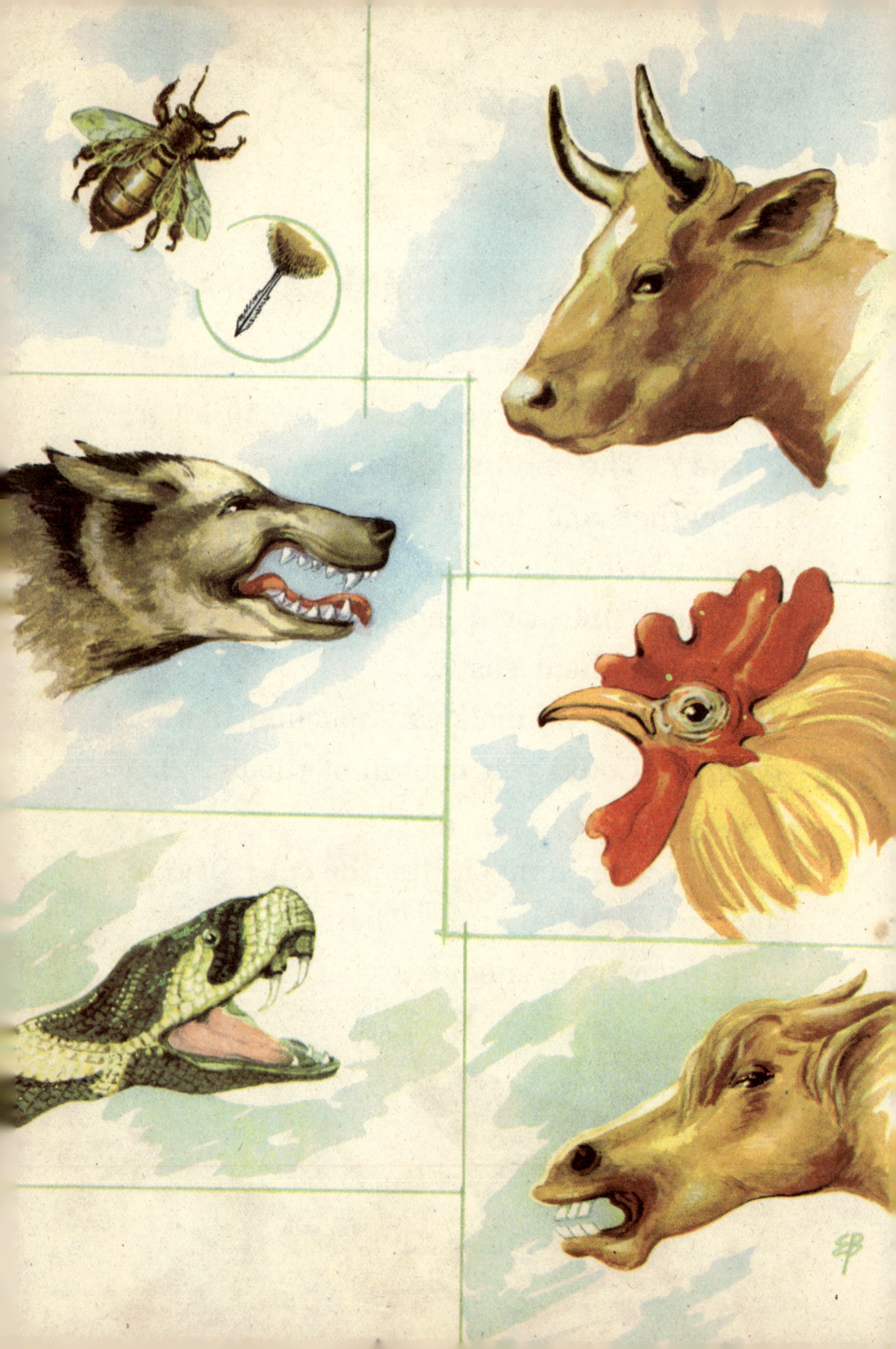

Each of these animals has something with which to fight its enemies. Some animals fight with more than one part of the body.

These animals have coverings that help to keep them safe from their enemies.

These animals do not need to be afraid. They have such a bad taste that other animals do not like them for food. Most animals will not eat them.

Some animals cannot fight. Their bodies are not made for fighting. Enemies can bite through their covering. What is their way of keeping safe?

A Question Box

You will not find the answers to these questions in the story. But the story will help you to think them out for yourself.

1. Which animal gets its food more easily?

A chickadee which eats small seeds, or
A lion which catches a zebra for food?

2. Which animal is better off in winter?

A beaver which sleeps in its own warm home, or
A blue jay which hides in the evergreen trees when it storms?

3. Which animal has the better way of keeping safe from its enemies?

A wolf which fights its enemies, or
A rabbit which runs away from them?

4. Each animal has a way of taking care of itself. Is one way better than another?

Animal Homes

Where is your home? Is it on a sunny street in a small town? Do you live in a farmhouse in the country? Or is your home at the seashore?

Many people live in homes that are high in the air. Some apartment houses reach up, up, up above the city streets. Do you live in a high apartment house?

People make their homes in all kinds of places on the earth. As you look about, you can find many other kinds of homes.

Homes on the Ground

You can find the homes of many animals on the ground at your feet.

Rabbits make nests on the ground in the fields. These nests are homes for their young.

Almost always the mother rabbit puts her nest where other animals cannot find it easily. She finds a place in the high grass. The nest often is near a fence or under some bushes.

The grass makes a soft place for the baby rabbits. The mother pulls hair from her body. This does not hurt her. The hair would come out anyway. She spreads the hair on the grass for a nest.

The young rabbits stay close to the nest until they can care for themselves. Their fur is the color of the dry grass. The thick high grass makes a good home for rabbits.

Homes under the Ground

Suppose you had eyes that could look down into the ground. Suppose you could see what is in the ground in your yard. You would find the homes of hundreds of little animals.

You would see the homes of ants. You would see the homes of some wasps and some spiders. You would see the homes of beetles and cutworms.

If you could look into the ground you would see earthworms making their long holes.

If you could look into the ground, you would see the homes of chipmunks.

On a sunny day in fall, try to find some chipmunks at work. Look for them near an old stone wall. Look for them in a field near the woods.

Chipmunks run about getting their home ready for winter. They find grain and other seeds. They find acorns and other nuts.

They hurry, hurry! They run with the food in their mouths. They hide it away under stones, or in any good hole they can find.

Then they dig, dig, dig. They make long tunnels under the ground. They dig away the ground to make two rooms. One is a storeroom. The other is the nest.

The chipmunks go into the rooms through one tunnel. They can go away from the rooms through two or three tunnels.

A small hole is the doorway to the tunnel that goes to the nest. It is not easy to find the doorway in the thick grass. The back doorways are hidden away even more carefully.

At last the tunnels and rooms are ready. The chipmunks look around for the nuts and other food they have stored away. They take this down to the storeroom.

The chipmunks take grass and dry leaves into the other room. This room is the nest. The chipmunks will curl up and rest in this room when cold winter comes.

Now the home is ready for winter. Chipmunks rest in the nest when days are cold. They eat when they are hungry.

On a warm winter day they may come up above the ground. But they go back as soon as cold weather comes again.

This home is a good place in winter. The chipmunks are away from cold and snow. They are away from most of their enemies.

By spring baby chipmunks will be living in the nest, too.

Homes in Water

Water makes a good home for many animals. Fish live all the time in their water homes.

Some animals build their homes in water. Muskrats make very fine winter homes in water. They find quiet water in a pool or brook. They work together to make a pile of sticks, leaves, and roots.

Inside the pile a place is left for a large room. The muskrats will live in this room.

Part of the pile is in the water. Part of it is above the water. The room where the muskrats live is above the water.

The door to the house is a tunnel. The tunnel goes down from the floor into the water. When the muskrats leave the house, they go into the tunnel. Then they swim out into the water.

In winter muskrats spend much of their time sleeping in this house. They eat when they wake up. Then they go back to sleep again.

They eat the food that they stored in their houses in the autumn. Sometimes they even eat some of the small sticks that their houses are made of. They can catch fish in the winter time. They find other food in the water, too.

The muskrats' home is good for them. It is built in a good place for their ways of living.

Homes near the Ground

Have you seen yellow warblers flying near your home? Have you heard their bright songs? Look for a warbler's nest in bushes near your home.

Many warblers and song sparrows make their nests in bushes. Catbirds and many other birds build in bushes, too.

These nests are near the ground. They are away from enemies that live in high trees. They are away from some of their enemies that live on the ground.

Homes in Trees

High trees are the homes of many, many animals. Such trees are something like apartment houses. There are homes in the big branches and in the little branches. There are homes in the tiptop of the tree. There are homes in the trunk.

Many birds build their nests in the big branches. Here you will find the nests of robins, king birds, and blue jays.

Young gray squirrels, too, live in the branches. Their home is a nest made of sticks and leaves. It is placed far out on the branches away from the trunk.

It does not look like a strong nest. But somehow or other it stays together. It makes a good home for young squirrels.

This nest is a summer home for gray squirrels. Their winter home is in the trunk of the tree. The squirrels curl up there and rest when the weather is cold.

Other animals live in tree trunks, too. Woodpeckers nest in the trunks of trees. Have you heard them tapping on the tree? They make holes in the trunk with their bills.

As the woodpecker taps, the hole gets bigger. Little pieces of wood fall down into the tree. These little pieces of wood make the nest soft for the young woodpeckers.

Crows build their nests high in the tops of trees. They build in the highest places they can find.

Eagles, too, sometimes make their nests in the tiptop of the highest trees.

The eagles' nest is like a platform. It is made of small sticks. It looks as if the eagles just threw the sticks together.

Homes in High Rocky Places

Some eagles make their homes high up on rocky mountainsides. They find a small flat place on the side of the rock. On one side of the nest the rock goes up, up, up. On the other side, the rock goes down, down, down.

There is little room to walk about near the nest. The young eagles are not afraid to fly from this high nest. They are at home high in the air.

Sea birds called gannets make homes on high rocks. The rocks are high up over the waves of the sea.

Gannets find small flat places on the side of the rock as some eagles do. They make their nests of seaweed. Hundreds of gannets build nests near to each other.

The homes of gannets and eagles are away from most of their enemies.

The rocky top of a mountain is a good home for mountain sheep. Not many men can get to this home. They cannot climb over the rocks.

But mountain sheep climb about over these rocks. They find good places to walk. They jump from one rock to another. Away they go over rocks that men cannot climb.

A little grass grows on the mountain top. The sheep eat the grass. In winter they come down the mountain to the woods.

As soon as spring comes, they go back to the top of the mountain. They stay there until the snow flies.

Animals make their homes in all kinds of places. Each place is a good home for the animal that lives there.

What Are Homes Made Of?

What is your house made of? What about the homes of other children in your school? One of you may live in a house made of wood. Another may live in a stone house. What other things are used in building people's homes?

These pictures tell about animal homes in fields and woods. What things do these animals use to make their homes?

The homes of some animals are made of wood.

The homes of some caterpillars and spiders are made of silk.

Some wasps make a home of paper. The paper is made with something that comes from the body of the wasp.

Some animals have homes made of stone. This insect covers itself with small stones which are held together with silk from the body. It lives in water.

Some swallows and some wasps use mud to make their homes.

Grasses, hair, paper, leaves, string, feathers, small sticks, and roots — all these are used by birds for their homes.

Animals use whatever they have to build their homes. Each kind of animal uses something which makes a good home for that animal.

Carefully Built Homes

Animals make many different kinds of homes. Is one of these homes better than another?

The Baltimore oriole is one of the finest builders in the world. Baltimore orioles nest in high trees. They build their nests at the very end of a high branch.

They take long dry grasses. They find pieces of string and horse hair. They use long strings from the stems of milkweed plants. They make these into a deep nest which hangs from the branch like a bag.

The birds tie the string and grasses round and round the branch. This holds the top of the nest in place.

The bottom of the nest is bigger around than the top. The eggs lie deep in the bottom of the nest. When the baby birds come from the eggs, they stay at the bottom of the nest.

The wind swings the nest about. It rocks the birds in the nest, but they do not fall out. Look at the picture of a Baltimore oriole's nest. Can you tell why the birds do not fall out when the nest swings in the wind?

Have you ever seen hummingbirds at work? They move ever so quickly. Their wings make a humming sound as they fly among the flowers in the garden.

A hummingbird's nest is one of the prettiest homes you can find. It is one of the tiniest that you can see.

Hummingbirds use the finest, softest things that grow for their nest. They put them together in a wonderful way.

The nest is just big enough to hold two tiny eggs. When it is finished, it looks like a part of the branch. How is this a help to the baby hummingbirds?

Quickly Built Homes

Not all birds are such fine builders as the Baltimore oriole and the hummingbird. Here is a nighthawk on its nest. The next page shows a whippoorwill on its nest. What do you think of these nests?

The nighthawk sometimes lays her eggs on the ground. Sometimes she lays them on the flat roof of a building.

The nighthawk does not make a nest. She uses only a little sand or some small stones. All she needs is a place where the eggs will not roll away.

The eggs are spotted. They look like the place where they are laid. The young birds have gray spots. They look like the sand and the stones on the ground.

It is not easy for the nighthawk's enemies to see the eggs or the baby birds. Nighthawks do not need a better nest.

The whippoorwill takes a little more time to make a nest. She puts two or three dry leaves together on the ground in the woods. These make her nest.

The mother whippoorwill lays two eggs. They have big light-colored spots which make them look like the dry leaves.

You could walk by this nest without seeing it. Do you think the whippoorwill makes a good kind of nest?

This Is a Good Home

Some insects make nests. They lay eggs too, but they do not sit on the eggs as birds do.

This is the nest of the mason wasp. Did you know that an insect could make a home like this?

First the mother mason wasp flies about to find some mud. She takes a little mud back to the tree. She gets more mud and more mud. She puts the mud together to make the nest.

This nest will be the home of just one mason wasp. When the nest is finished, the mother lays one egg. The egg hangs from the top of the nest.

Next, the mother wasp looks for some caterpillars. She stings the caterpillars and carries them into the nest.

Then she puts a cover over the top of the nest. A little white larva will come out of the egg. It will eat the caterpillars. It will have enough food to make it grow and grow.

The mother mason wasp makes many of these little nests. Then she flies away. The care of her young is ended.

Many moths and butterflies lay eggs on plants. Food is ready for the larvae which come out of the eggs. They will eat the leaves of the plant. The plant is home for the young caterpillars.

No Homes

May flies do not give even this much care to their young. May flies fly out over a pool or a river and drop their eggs into the water. Then they fly back to the land.

The water makes a good enough home for young May flies. Many of them come out of the eggs. Many live to grow up.

Many fish give their young no more care than May flies do. Salmon lay their eggs in the water. They lay ever so many eggs — more than you can count. Then they swim away.

Many of the salmon eggs are eaten by other fish. But hundreds and hundreds and hundreds of salmon live to grow up.

Some fish do a little to make a nest for eggs. As you know, the father sunfish watches the eggs until the fish come out.

Many kinds of fish and other animals make no homes for their young. But many, many of these kinds of animals live on in the world.

Now, think again about this question. Is one kind of home better than another?

Some homes are made with great care. Some are made with little care. Some animals make no homes for their young.

Some animals need much care. Baby orioles must have a well built home. They cannot care for themselves. The mother oriole cares for them until they are grown up.

May flies, salmon, and many other insects and fish do not need homes. They do not need a mother's care. They take care of themselves as soon as they are out of the eggs.

Each kind of home is a good home for the animal that makes it.

What Are Homes For?

What does your home do for you?

Your home is the place where you keep warm in winter. Your home keeps you safe from rain and snow and freezing wind.

Home is the place where you sleep and eat. It is the place where you work and play. It is a place where your friends come to visit.

Home is the place that your father and mother make for you. It is the place where they take care of you.

Most animals have some place to get away from rain and wind and snow. But all animals do not use their homes in the same ways.

Some animals use their homes to get away from cold winter. Which animals that you have read about make this use of their homes? Tell about other animals that go into the ground for the winter.

Some homes are used to store away food. What animals make a place for food in their homes?

Some homes are a place to hold the young. Birds make nests to hold the eggs and the young birds. When the young birds no longer need the nest, it is not used for a home.

Grown-up birds do not use the nest to get away from wind and rain. They find other places to go. The nest is just a bed for the young birds.

See for Yourself

1. Look about you for animal homes. You may find a caterpillar under a leaf. You may find a woodpecker's hole in a tree. You may find a hole which a rabbit uses to get away from storms.

2. Look around cornstalks that are piled up in a field. Mice, birds, and other small animals go into the dry cornstalks.

3. Find different kinds of animal homes. Find the home of a spider, an earthworm, or an ant. Why is each home good for the kind of animal that lives in it?

4. Look about you for an apartment house for animals. Yellow jacket wasps make a fine apartment house. Do not look into the house when you first see it. Find out if any yellow jackets are at home. If you know that every wasp is gone, then take a quick look inside.

Be a Builder Yourself

1. Make a house which birds can use for a home. You can make a small house for a wren. You can make a bigger house for a bluebird. Put the house in a place where the birds can find it.

2. Make a feeding box for birds to use in winter. Find out what foods they like. Keep this food where the birds can get it.

3. Put a pan of water in your yard for birds. Find a good place for the pan. Put it where the birds will not be afraid to use it. What do they use it for?

4. Find a bird's nest that is no longer used. Look at it carefully. Find out what it is made of. Try to see just how it was made.

5. Try to make a bird's nest yourself. Do you think you ever could make a nest as a bird can?

What a Magnet Can Do

Playing with Magnets

Many children have magnets for toys. It is real fun to play with a magnet. Even grown-up people like to see what a magnet can do.

Put a small nail across the ends of a magnet. Now hold the magnet any way you want to. Hold it right side up, or upside down. Swing it around and around. The nail stays on the magnet.

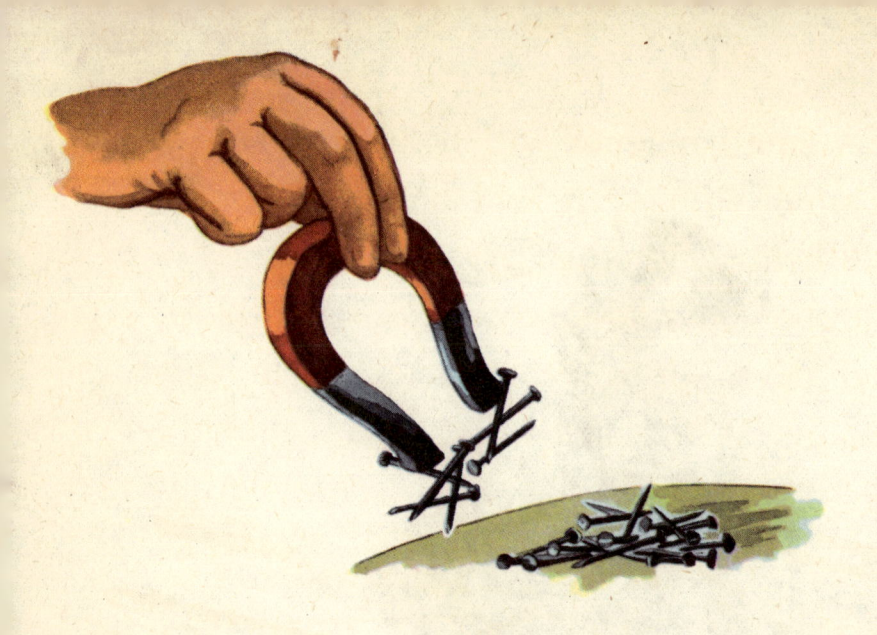

The nail comes off the magnet when someone pulls it off. It does not drop off. The magnet pulls the nail to itself.

Try to find some nails about as long as this:

Make a pile of twenty or thirty of these nails on your desk. Push the ends of the magnet into the pile of nails.

Now take the magnet out of the pile of nails. Many of these small nails stay on the magnet. Count to see how many nails the magnet will hold.

A small magnet will hold many kinds of small things. It will hold needles. It will hold some pins.

Put on your desk some pins, a small key, and other things that you see in this picture. Which ones will the magnet hold?

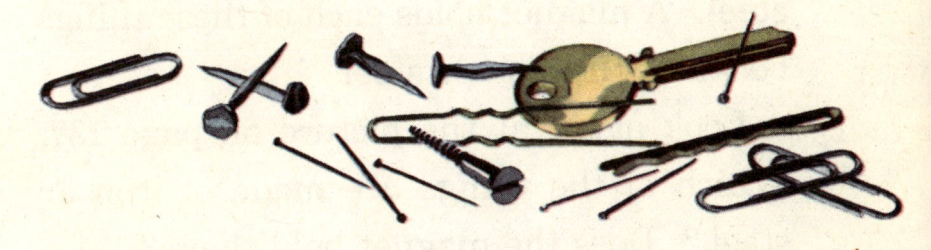

Some things will not stay on a magnet. Try a piece of paper. Try a gold ring. Try a ribbon and a piece of string.

What happens to these things when you try to put them on the magnet?

Now you know that a magnet will hold some things, and that it will not hold others.

Do you know what a nail is made of? It is made of iron or steel. A needle is made of steel. Some pins are made of steel. A magnet holds each of these things because it is iron or steel.

Look again at the picture on page 137. Which of the things are made of iron or steel? Does the magnet hold them?

The magnet does not hold things that are not made of iron or steel. The ring is made of gold. The magnet will not hold a gold ring.

It will not hold the paper or the string or the ribbon. It will not hold some of the pins. These things are not made of iron or steel.

The magnet pulls to itself things that are made of iron and steel.

The Pull of a Magnet

One day David said, "I can make this magnet hold a piece of paper."

"A magnet cannot hold paper," said Ann. "Paper is not made of iron or steel."

"Just watch and see," said David. "Jack, you hold the magnet."

Jack held the magnet. David put a piece of paper under the magnet. He placed a nail under the paper.

Click! The nail and the paper held fast to the magnet.

What do you think? Did the magnet really hold the paper?

The pull of a magnet goes through paper.

Put a needle on a piece of paper. Hold a magnet under the paper. Move the magnet round and round under the paper. Watch the needle go round and round on top of the paper.

The magnet pulls the needle. The pull of the magnet goes through the paper. As the magnet is moved about under the paper, the needle moves around on top of the paper.

Now what do you think about David's trick? What made the paper stay on the magnet?

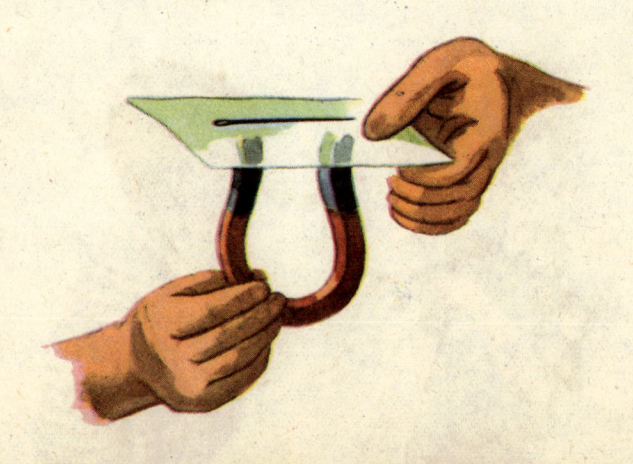

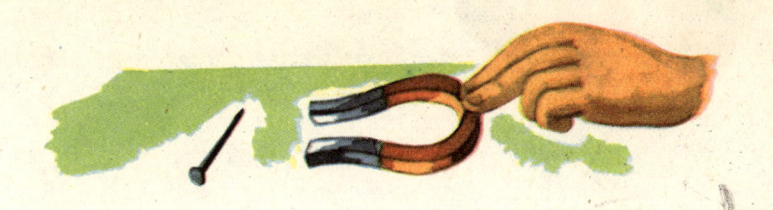

The pull of a magnet goes through air. Place a nail on your desk. Place a magnet on the desk, too. Move the magnet along until it is near the nail. Move it very slowly. When the magnet is very near to the nail, click! the nail hops over to the magnet.

The pull of the magnet goes through the air to the nail. The nail hops through the air over to the magnet.

Does the pull of a magnet go through water? Drop a needle into a glass of water. Put a magnet in the water to get the needle.

Can the magnet take the needle out of the water?

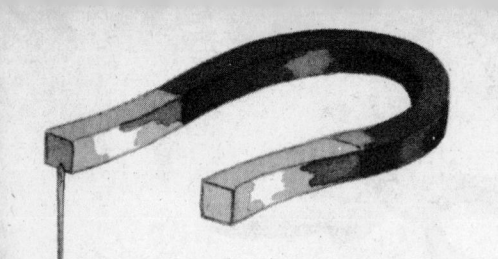

How Much Will a Magnet Hold?

Jack took a large needle. He placed it at the end of a magnet.

He took a second needle. He put the eye of this needle at the point of the first needle. He took a third needle. He put the eye of this needle at the point of the second needle. He took a fourth needle. He put the eye of this needle at the point of the third needle. Four needles were on the magnet.

"Now watch," said Jack. He took the first needle from the magnet. Down dropped all the other needles.

It is fun to find out how many things a magnet can pull to itself.

Just for Fun

Can you make a boat sail on the water without any wind? You will need these things to do the trick:

    Some corks   Some needles
    Some paper   A magnet

Make a little boat out of paper. Cut a small sail out of paper.

Put the needle through the paper sail as you see it in the picture.

Stick the point of the needle into a cork. Next put the cork with its sail into the boat.

Now your boat is ready to sail in a pan of water. The cork will make the boat float on top of the water.

Hold a magnet near the boat. It will pull the boat along. It will take the boat anywhere you want it to go.

The World Uses Electricity

All through the day and all through the night, electricity works for you.

Try to count the ways that electricity helps you. How many ways there are! Do you think you can count all of them?

Electricity Gives Light

At night city streets are bright with light. You hardly know it is night until you look up at the dark sky. All over the city people are using electric lights.

Many people work at night. Electricity helps them to see to do their work. What kinds of work do people do at night?

People can see to do many things very well at night. They do not need to wait for daytime to do some of their work.

In the pictures below two boys are trying to read by electric light. You do not need to be told which boy has the better light.

When you read or study, you should use the best light you can get. You should take good care of your eyes. Poor light is not good for your eyes.

Electricity Helps with Work

Many machines are run by electricity. Some of them are in people's homes. How many can you see in the picture on pages 144–145? These machines help to make housework easy.

Many, many of the things people use every day are made in factories. Shoes, caps, dresses, suits, coats, leggings, chairs, beds, tables, dishes—hundreds of things are made in factories. In many of these factories, the machines are run by electricity

Fred lives in the city. Wherever he goes, electricity helps him to travel. An electric elevator takes him from his apartment to the street floor. An electric elevator takes him up and down in the big city buildings.

Sometimes Fred rides downtown on an electric streetcar. When he goes to visit his grandmother he rides on an electric train.

Electricity helps people on farms, too. Everyone in the Davis family is glad electricity has come to their farm.

Look again at the picture on pages 144–145. Mrs. Davis has all of those things to help her with her work. An electric pump sends water to the house.

She often says, "Housework is much easier than it used to be."

The pump sends water to the barnyard, too. Peter says, "The pump makes it easier to water the cows and chickens."

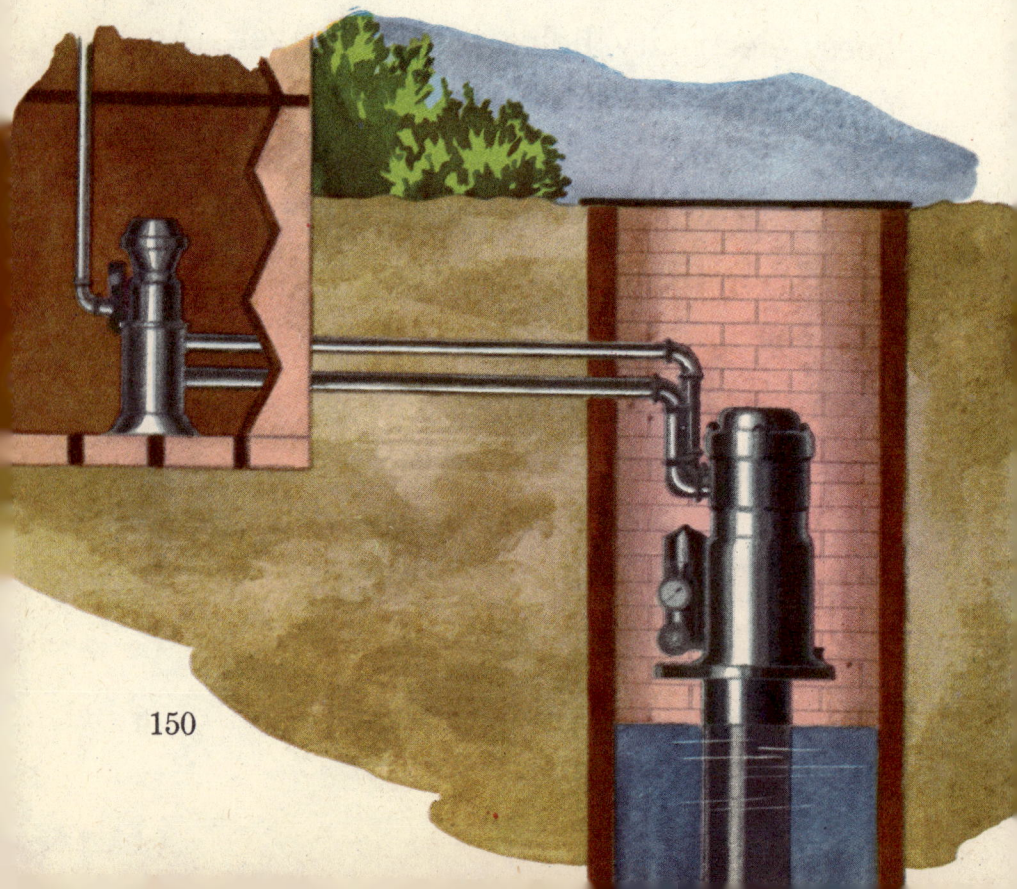

Mr. Davis says, "The electric milking machine is wonderful. It milks all the cows in a very short time."

Electricity is a help to many farmers like Mr. Davis.

In the city and in the country, in factories and on farms, electricity helps people with their work.

Electricity Spreads the News

By radio we learn what people are doing in all parts of the world. Some radio talks come to us from far, far away. But we hear the words as soon as they are said.

The telephone carries words as fast as the radio. How quickly your mother can talk with her friends in any part of town! How quickly she can call help when someone is hurt! How easily your father can talk with other men at work!

Over the ocean, across the land, around the world, words go traveling. Electricity sends them on their way.

Before people had telephones to use, they sent messages by telegraph. People today send messages by telegraph. This, too, is a quick way to send a message.

The man in the picture at the top of this page is sending a telegraph message. Electricity sends these messages on their way.

News from faraway places is sent us by telegraph, telephone, and radio. Words travel far and fast because we know how to use electricity. Without electricity, we might wait for days, weeks, or even years for news to reach us.

Electricity Comes to Your Town

It is night. Bob comes into a dark room. He pushes the button on the wall. At once the dark room is almost as light as day. Electricity has gone into the electric bulbs.

Bob's mother turns a button on the electric stove. Soon the burner on top of the stove is hot. Electricity has gone into the stove.

How does electricity get into a house?

Electricity does not stay in the wall. It is not waiting there for someone to push the button.

155

Electricity comes to homes from far away. It is sent out from a power house. Big machines are in the power house. These machines send out electric power for people to use.

Great wires go out from the power house. Electric power goes along these wires. The great wires take electric power to cities and farms. They take the electric power that helps the people in these places to live better. The wires take electric power to Your Town.

Wires go along the streets of Your Town. They may go under the street. In some towns you cannot see these wires. They are not in anyone's way when they are under the street.

Smaller wires go from the street into the houses. Wires go to all the rooms of the houses. Electricity goes through these wires. You push the button. Electricity comes to do its work.

No One Sees Electricity

All around you electricity is at work. You see what it does, but no one ever has seen electricity itself.

You cannot see electricity as it travels along a wire. If you could see inside the wire, you could not see electricity there.

No one sees electricity as it goes out from the power house. No one sees the electricity in a light bulb or an electric iron. You just see what electricity does. You see the light which electricity makes in the bulb. You feel the heat in the iron or the stove.

Electricity at Work

Not all electricity is sent out from a power house. You can get electricity in other ways. One of these ways is to use a dry cell.

← This is a post

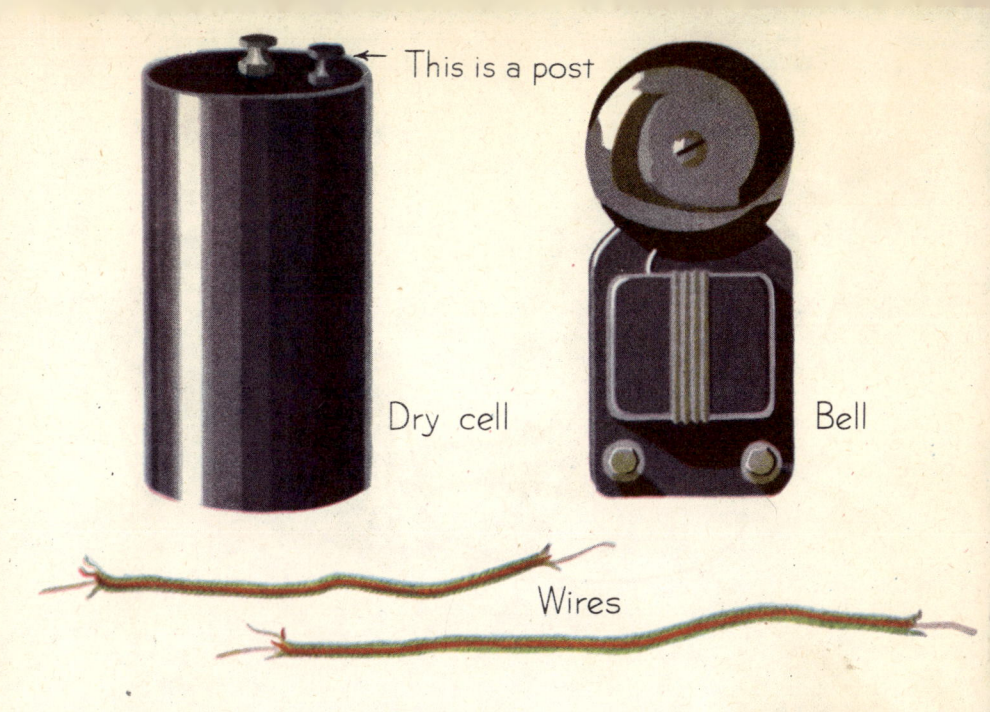

Dry cell

Bell

Wires

If you have a dry cell, you can watch electricity at work. You can make a bell ring. Find the picture of a dry cell at the top of the page. Do you see the two posts on the top?

Now find the picture of an electric bell. Do you see the posts under the box on the bell?

You will use all of these posts when you make the bell ring. Now you are ready to watch electricity at work.

Fasten the end of one wire around one post of the dry cell. Fasten the other end of the wire around one post on the bell.

Take the other wire. Fasten it to the other post of the dry cell and the other post of the bell.

Does the bell begin to ring? Does it ring and ring?

How can you make the bell stop ringing? Just take one end of one of the wires away from the post. Then the bell cannot ring.

Electricity Travels along a Pathway

Electricity travels. It travels from the power house to you.

It travels from the dry cell to the bell and makes it ring.

How does electricity travel? It goes along a pathway. You can find a pathway for electricity.

Look at the picture. Do you see the path which electricity takes?

Electricity goes to the bell through the wires. It must go to the bell along one wire. It must come back to the dry cell along the other wire.

Electricity goes around and around on its pathway. It always comes back to the place from which it started.

An electric bell will ring because the electricity has a pathway. The wires, the cell, and the bell make a pathway for the electricity.

Take off one of the wires that go from the dry cell to the bell. It will look like the picture.

Now the bell will not ring. Something has happened to the pathway.

Electricity cannot go from the end of the wire through the air to the bell. The wires must be fastened so that they make a pathway for electricity.

Use Electricity with Care

The children in Miss Snow's room were learning about electricity. They learned how to make a bell ring and how to do other things with electricity.

These children knew that electricity from the dry cells would not hurt them. But they always were careful when they used the dry cells.

One day Miss Snow said, "Electricity is a great help to people. But they should be careful when they use it. Sometimes it can hurt people who are not careful."

The children talked about good ways to use electricity.

They said, "We should show other people how to be careful when they use electricity."

Then they made a sign. On the next page, you will see their sign.

Watch Out for Electricity

1. Always turn off electricity as soon as you have finished using it.

2. Never turn on electricity when your hands are wet.

3. Never turn on electricity when you are touching water in any way.

4. Be careful of electric lights. Never put your hand into the place where the light bulb goes. Never put anything into the place where the electricity comes out.

5. Sometimes you may see long wires in the street. Keep away from them. Never touch them. They may be electric wires.

Electricity and Good Times

It is night, but the people in the picture can see to swim very well.

Electric lights help many people to play out of doors at night. Have you ever watched people playing out of doors at night? What were they playing?

Electricity helps many people to have a good time. Have you ever had a ride on a merry-go-round?

Do you like to go to a moving picture show? Moving picture machines are run by electricity.

Have you played with an electric train? Have you played with other toys that are run by electricity? Electricity helps you to have fun in many ways.

Something to Make

You can make a fine book about the uses of electricity.

1. Tell some of the ways in which you use electricity every day.

2. Make a picture of the way electric wires go into your house.

3. Make a picture to show how to wire an electric bell.

4. Find pictures of these things.
Many kinds of electric lights.
Ways in which electricity is used for heat.
Ways in which electricity is used to make things move.
Ways in which electricity is used to send messages on their way.

5. Paste these pictures in your book. Your book will be a good story of electricity.

We Live in Air

People Travel by Air

Bob and his mother and father stepped out of the car at the airport. The day was cloudy and dark. Fog was over the city and around the airport.

People were getting into the plane.

"Can we start out in this weather?" Mr. Baker asked the pilot.

"The weather man says to go ahead," answered the pilot.

Soon the airplane was off the ground. Up through the fog it climbed. Up, up, up it went through the rain clouds over the city of New Town.

The plane climbed higher and higher and higher. Then Bob had a big surprise. Bright sunshine was coming through the windows. Bright sunshine was all around them. Above them was blue sky.

"Look down, Bob," said his father.

Bob looked down. Under the airplane were clouds, clouds, clouds.

"It looks like a floor made of clouds," Bob said. The floor of clouds reached as far away as Bob could see.

"It is a floor that no one could walk upon," said Mr. Baker. "Not even birds or insects could walk upon that floor."

But Bob did not see any birds or insects. As the plane flew on and on, Bob thought, "We are alone up here in the sky."

Just then he saw another plane. The plane dipped its wings. Bob's plane dipped its wings. The two pilots were saying "Good morning" to each other up there in the sky.

By and by Bob asked, "How will the pilot know when we have reached East Town?"

"The radio will tell him," said Bob's mother. "When we are near the airport, it will tell him how to land the airplane."

Soon the co-pilot heard the radio at East Town calling him. The radio said, "Do not land at East Town. Low storms with wind. Go on to North Town."

So the airplane went on its way to North Town. It was high above the storm.

In a little while the radio at North Town called the co-pilot. It said, "Thick fog at North Town. Use care in landing."

Then the radio told the pilot just how to land the plane.

Down, down, down it came, out of the sunshine into the thick fog. Out of bright sunshine into a dark, wet day!

"That was a good trip for us," said the pilot. "We cannot always go above the clouds into sunshine. Sometimes the clouds are high up as well as near the earth. Then the planes may not leave the ground."

"How do we get to East Town?" Bob asked. "Can we get there today?"

"Yes," Mr. Baker answered. "We can get to East Town today. But we must take the train. The weather has grounded us."

Some Great Air Travelers

For many hundreds of years, people have been living on the earth. For most of those long years, they have had to stay on the ground.

Birds and insects could go up in the air. They have been flying as long as they have been living on the earth.

People always have wanted to fly, too. But they had to stay on the ground. At last they learned to make machines that could travel in air. Now people can fly across oceans and around the world.

An airplane is a wonderful machine. But birds and insects can fly without a machine. They can go up into the air on their own power. A little flap with their wings and away they go! Off the ground! Up in the air! Up as high as they need to go!

Birds and insects can go up into the air at any time. They do not need to wait until it is time for the airplane to start. A flap of their wings and they are off!

Many birds and insects could not get food if they could not fly.

Suppose a robin or a bluebird could not fly to places where its food is found. How would they get from the branches to the ground? How would they get back to their nests in the trees? How would they carry food to their baby birds in the nests?

Many birds find their food high in the treetops. Swallows and some other birds catch insects as they fly through the air. Sea gulls fly over the water and dive for fish. Most birds could not live if they could not fly to get food. They could not feed the young birds in the nest.

Eagles fly to nests that are high up on a mountain. Sea gulls follow ships on the ocean for miles and miles.

Have you ever heard of a small sea bird called the stormy petrel? Petrels fly out over the ocean for food. They catch fish in the stormy waves. Petrels fly into storms that the pilot of an airplane would not like to meet. Do you think stormy petrel is a good name for this bird?

In spring and fall many birds travel a long way. How far a swallow flies when it goes south for the winter!

Today people fly in airplanes to all parts of the earth. But birds and insects traveled in air long, long before people learned to fly.

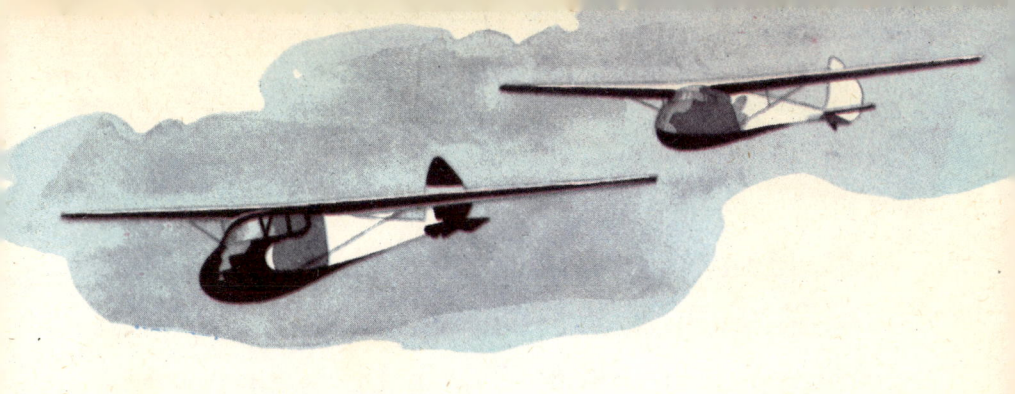

Things Sail in Air

High on a windy hill children go to fly their kites. Higher and higher sail the kites. They go as far as the string will let them go.

Boats sail on water. Kites sail in air. They sail away in the wind.

Some airplanes sail in air too. These airplanes do not have engines. Some of them are called gliders. Some are called sail planes.

Someone has to get these planes into the air at first. Like kites they must get up into the wind. A glider is pulled along by another plane. A sail plane can glide by itself for many miles through the air.

Eagle   Gull   Robin

Many animals sail in the air. Eagles and gulls travel for many miles without stopping to rest. These birds do not use their wings as smaller birds do. They do not flap their wings up and down all the time. Many times they just glide in the air.

The wings of gulls and eagles are wide, with long feathers. They use their wide wings for sailing. They glide and dip and sail around and around in the air. They sometimes flap their wings. But much of the time their wings move just enough to make them glide where they need to go.

Many insects sail in the air. Mosquitoes cannot fly very far with their tiny wings, but they can sail far through the air. The wind often takes them miles away from the place where they have been living.

Have you ever seen a flying squirrel? Look at the skin at each side of the body. Do you think a flying squirrel really flies?

You have seen many gray squirrels with long bushy tails. What long jumps they take through the trees! A gray squirrel's tail is like a sail. The squirrel glides a little as it jumps through the air. The air helps him to take these long jumps.

Many things glide through the air. Watch the air when you are out of doors. How many " air gliders " can you see?

Now You See Water in the Air Now You Don't

When Bob Baker took his airplane ride, fog covered the ground.

Sometimes fog comes to the place where you live. It is all around your house. It is in the streets. Wherever you look, you see fog. Your face feels wet when you walk in the fog. Everything around you feels wet.

Fog is water in the air. It is water that you can see.

Fog is a cloud. Fog is a cloud that is near the ground. Most clouds are high in the air. When you look at these clouds you are seeing water in the air.

Watch a pan of vegetables when they are boiling on the stove. Do you see a little cloud just above the pan? This is water that you can see in the air.

The water cloud above the pan soon evaporates into the air. Then it is water that you cannot see.

Water goes into the air from many places. Much of the water which is in the air cannot be seen.

When you paint a picture, at first the paint is wet. Then the wet paint dries. You know that the water has evaporated into the air, but you cannot see it there.

The sidewalks are wet after a rain. Then the sun shines and in a short time the sidewalks are dry. The water has evaporated into the air.

Sometimes you can see a little cloud above the sidewalk. But almost always the water goes into the air without your seeing it there.

Look all about you. Find many things that are drying. The water goes from all of these things into the air.

Heat Makes Water Go into the Air

Watch Mother as she irons a dress with a hot iron. At first the dress is wet. When Mother has finished ironing it, the dress is dry.

In winter where do you put your wet mittens to dry? Where do you put your wet swimming suit in summer? What dries your mittens and your swimming suit?

Heat from the sun dries the sidewalks quickly after a rain. It dries puddles in the streets.

Mother watches the boiling vegetables. Heat from the stove makes the water boil away. All the water must not boil away into the air. The vegetables will burn if all the water boils away.

Heat makes water go into the air.

Water Comes Out of the Air

Some of the water that goes into the air comes back where you can see it.

Look at the window in the room where the vegetables are boiling. Do you see drops of water on the window?

Where did these drops of water come from? Is it raining outside? Did they come through the window? No, the drops of water came from the air inside the kitchen.

The air in the kitchen is warm. The window glass is cold. The air holds much water that you cannot see. The warm air meets the cold glass. Some of the water comes out of the air onto the glass.

One winter day, Grandfather came to visit Ann. He took off his hat. Then he took off his glasses.

"Now, I can see you," he said to Ann.

Ann said, "I should think you could see me better with your glasses on."

"Right now I cannot see through my glasses at all," Grandfather told her.

What had happened to Grandfather's glasses? When he first came into the warm house, his glasses were cold. Soon they were covered with drops of water.

The water came out of the air. It came out of the warm air onto Grandfather's cold glasses. Grandfather could not see. So he took off his glasses.

By and by Grandfather put on his glasses. "Now I can see you more clearly with my glasses on," he said.

The glasses had become as warm as the room. The little drops of water had gone back into the air.

Heat makes water go into the air. Cold makes water come out of the air.

On a warm day put some pieces of ice and a little water into a small pan. Stir the ice around. Soon you will see little drops of water on the outside of the pan.

Where do these drops of water come from? At first the air around the pan was warm. The ice in the pan was cold. The cold pan made the water come out of the air. The water made little drops on the outside of the pan.

Let the pan stand in a warm place until the ice melts. By and by you will not see the drops of water on the outside of the pan. What has happened to them?

Now you see water in air! Now you don't!

Can You Tell?

When Bob came in from swimming, he dropped his suit in a pile on the ground.

"Spread out your suit, Bob," said his mother. "It will dry better that way."

Bob wants the water to evaporate from his suit. He must place his suit so that air can reach all parts of it.

In which way will air reach all parts of Bob's suit so that it will dry fast?

Using Thermometers

In many parts of the earth the air is very, very hot. Around noon it is so hot that people stay in the house if they can. They try to keep out of the burning sunshine. It is very hot even in the shade. Dogs lie still with their tongues out. Donkeys stand quietly until someone makes them move.

Some places on the earth have very cold winters. When people go out of doors, they wear their warmest coats. They cover their ears. Sometimes they cover their faces.

Before going out someone may ask, "How cold is it?"

"Watch out!" comes the answer. "This cold air can freeze your nose and ears before you know it."

How can you tell that the air is very cold in the picture on page 189? How can you tell that it is very hot in the picture on page 188?

Sometimes you want to know just how warm a place is or how cold it is. You want to know the temperature of the place. Do you know how to find the temperature? Learn to use a thermometer.

Look at a thermometer at school or at home. Find the red line on it. Heat makes the red line climb up. Cold sends the red line down.

Put the thermometer in a warm place. Watch the red line go up. Find the number at the end of the red line. This number tells how high the temperature is.

Put the thermometer in a cold place. Watch the red line go down. Find the number at the end of the red line. This number tells how low the temperature is.

The numbers on a thermometer are called degrees. We use degrees to tell temperature.

Find 0 on the thermometer. The air is very, very cold when the red line goes to 0. But air can be colder than 0. Look at the numbers below 0.

Look at the picture on page 189. Where these people live the red line on the thermometer goes down, down to 0. It may go to 40 degrees below 0.

In many, many parts of the earth the red line on the thermometer never goes down to 0. In some places it stays around 80 degrees. This is summer heat.

In some places, the red line on the thermometer never goes below 80. But it goes up, up, up! Look at the picture on page 188. Where these people live the red line climbs up and up to 90, 115, 120 degrees.

The thermometer which Mother puts in your mouth should go no higher than about 98 degrees. If it does, you are sick. You should go to bed.

Here are some degrees of temperature that children should know:

90 Very warm. Wear a sun suit.

70 The air in a room is about right. The air out of doors is warm. You need not wear a coat or cap.

60 Not very cold. But wear a coat or a jacket.

40 Not freezing cold. But wear a cap and a warm coat. What about leggings?

32 Water freezes at 32. When the red line stays well below 32 for two or three days ponds will freeze. Wear a warm coat, cap, mittens, leggings.

0 Very cold! When you go out of doors, wear your warmest clothes. If you go out to play, don't stay too long.

Some Things to Look For

1. Where have you seen thermometers? Do you have a thermometer outside a window at home? Can you see each morning how cold or how warm the air is?

2. Do you have a thermometer in the living room at home? Does it show about 70 degrees in winter?

3. Does Mother put a thermometer into your mouth when you are sick? What does a thermometer tell about a sick boy or girl?

4. Does your mother have a thermometer on her stove? It tells when the stove is just hot enough for baking a cake.

5. Try to find out which was the coldest day of the year where you live. How cold was the air on that day? Which day was the warmest day of the year? How warm was the air on that day?

Water for You and Me

Water Is Useful

Very often you say, "I want a drink of water."

And almost always you can have a drink of water when you want it.

But sometimes there is no water in the place where you are and you have to wait.

Then you do not feel very happy. You think, "I want a drink of water more than anything else in the world!"

You begin to think how very useful water is.

The children in Miss Black's room were talking about water.

Mary said, "We must have water to drink. We must have water for washing. We must have water for trees and gardens and all growing things."

Bill said, "There is water all around us. When it rains, we see water in the air. We often see clouds. Clouds are water."

Ann said, "Water is in lakes and rivers. The ocean is water."

Ben lives on a farm. Ben said, "There is water in the earth. The water comes into our house from a well. The well is a deep, deep hole in the ground. A pump brings the water up out of the ground. It runs into a tank in our house."

The children told many things about water.

Water is used in many ways, just as Mary said.

What would you do without water to drink? How would Mother get dinner without water? How could you keep clean without water?

Animals need water and so do plants.

Try to count the number of different ways that you use water in one day at home and at school.

Water in the Air

As Bill said, there is water in air. We see water when it rains.

We know that there is much water in air even when it is not raining. Water evaporates into the air all the time.

The wet washing on the line soon gets dry. After the rain stops, the grass soon dries. All wet places give up some of their water to the air.

Water on the Earth

As Ann said, there is much water on the earth, in oceans, lakes, and rivers.

Most of you can find running water in a brook or river. Watch the water as it runs along.

How much water runs by as you stand and look at it! Enough water to fill many tanks runs through a little brook in one day.

Try to find a map of the world in your room. The water on the map may be blue or green. The land part of the map is some other color. Look at the water part of the world. The map shows that there is more water than land on the earth.

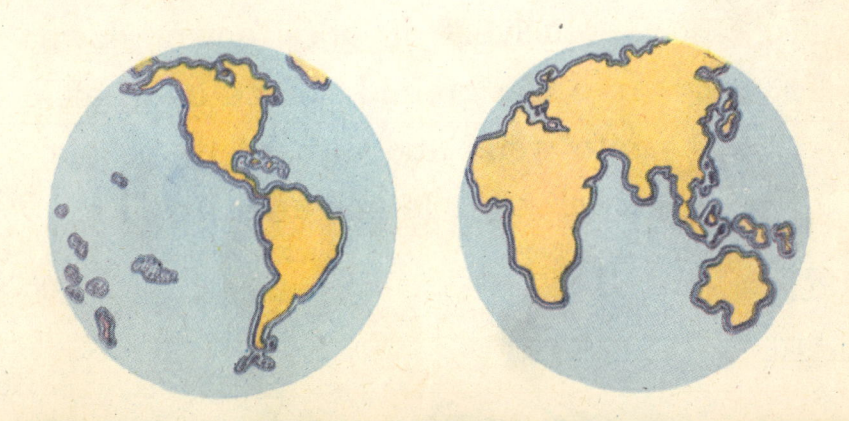

Water in the Ground

As Ben said, there is much water in the ground. Wells hold drinking water for people on most farms. Men dig deep into the ground to make wells.

After a hard rainstorm, look at the puddles of water in the yard or in the street. You do not see the puddles long after the rain is over.

Much of the water from the puddles goes into the ground. Here it is used by the roots of grass or trees. It is used by plants in the garden.

Much of it goes down, down into the ground. Some of it goes into wells and is used by people. Much of it is not used at all.

Water in Our Bodies

On hot days in summer time you take long drinks of water or lemonade.

Do you know why you need to drink so much water in summer? On hot days much water goes out of your body through your skin.

Is your body wet and sticky on hot days? Do little drops of water come out on your face?

Water, milk, and lemonade and other fruit drinks put water back into your body. Your body must have water.

In one way your body is like the earth. A great part of it is water. There is water in all parts of your body. You can see some of this water. Some of it you cannot see.

Water comes out through your skin when you are warm. What happens when you cry? Water comes out of your eyes. What happens when you have a cold? Water comes from your nose.

If you cut your hand, blood comes out. Much of your blood is water.

What about the water in your mouth? This water helps you to eat your food. How hard it would be to eat if your tongue and mouth were all dry!

There is much water in the bodies of all animals. Your dog looks very warm in summer. He likes to lie down. Some of the water from his body runs off his tongue.

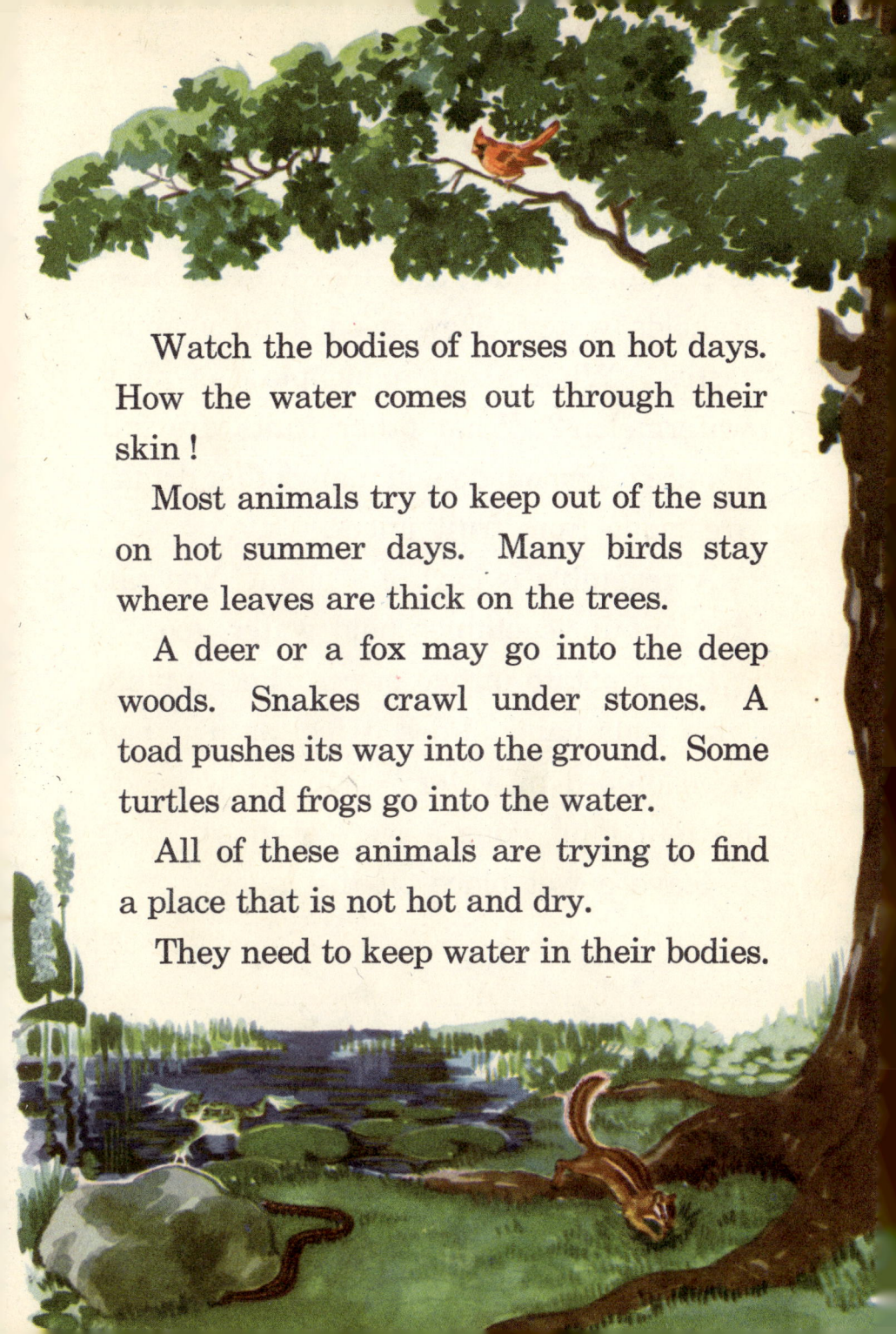

Watch the bodies of horses on hot days. How the water comes out through their skin!

Most animals try to keep out of the sun on hot summer days. Many birds stay where leaves are thick on the trees.

A deer or a fox may go into the deep woods. Snakes crawl under stones. A toad pushes its way into the ground. Some turtles and frogs go into the water.

All of these animals are trying to find a place that is not hot and dry.

They need to keep water in their bodies.

Water in Plants

You like to eat fruit in summer. Fruit is part of a plant. You like fruit because it holds water. How good a juicy apple tastes! What about a big piece of juicy watermelon? What other fruits are full of juice? Lemonade and many other drinks are made from fruit juices.

A vegetable is part of a plant. You can find out if vegetables hold water, too.

Cut a potato in two pieces. Feel a piece with your hand. Does it feel as if it had been dipped in water? Rub the wet side of the potato along a piece of glass. Does it leave a wet place on the glass?

Cut a slice from the potato. Put it on a paper. Make a line around the slice of potato. This will show how large the slice is.

Leave the piece of potato in a dry place. In a day or two it will be very dry. Put it on the paper where the line is. The slice of potato is much smaller than it was at first. It is smaller because much of the water has gone out of it.

When Water Is a Help

Water is a great help to all the people who live upon the earth.

From earliest days, people have used boats for travel. On rivers, lakes, and oceans they have gone to faraway places.

Water puts many great machines to work. It runs many of the great machines in power houses. These machines send out electricity.

You know that water can be changed to steam. Have you seen a steam engine pulling a long train of cars? Steam gives the engine power to pull the train.

You know that the steam comes from boiling water. You know what part of the engine holds the water which turns into steam. Steam has great power.

People have done many things on this earth because they have had water to use.

Water helps many animals because it gives them a place to live.

Small sunfish and great whales live in water. Many animals stay in water much of the time.

Muskrats and beavers build fine homes in water.

Many turtles, frogs, and snakes live near water. Their food comes from the water. Their bodies need water.

Plants, too, must have water. They grow where there is water. Not many plants are found in places where there is little water.

The roots of some plants go deep into the ground to find water.

Sometimes the ends of the roots are far away from the top of the plant. They are growing to a place that has water.

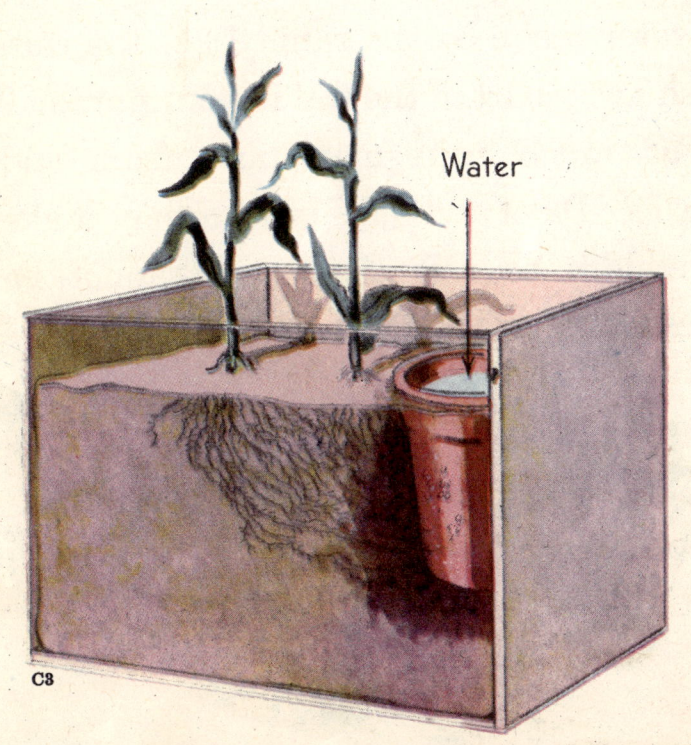

Water

When Water Does Not Help

Sometimes water does not help living things. It hurts them.

Too much rain does not help a garden. It may wash away the seeds you have just planted. It may wash away young plants that have just started to grow.

Look at the ground as the rain comes down. Watch the puddles and little runs of water made by the rain. Does the rain wash away part of the soil in your garden?

Too much rain may hurt fruit and berries. Days and days of rain may make vegetables so soft that they cannot be eaten.

In some places spring may bring too much rain. Brooks and rivers have more water than they can hold. Then floods come to the land. Floods can be bad for many living things.

You know why floods are bad for people. In what ways are they bad for many animals? Why are floods bad for many plants?

Getting Water to People Who Need It

In many times and in many places, people have not had enough water. If it does not rain, food plants cannot grow. Cows, horses, and other animals do not have enough water to drink.

Dry times are hard times for people. But today, there are many ways for people to have water.

On a farm, water may be pumped from a well or it may be stored in a tank. People who live in cities get water that is stored in big tanks and reservoirs.

In the picture on pages 194 and 195 you can see a reservoir. This great reservoir holds water for more people than you can count. Very big cities have more than one of these reservoirs.

Sometimes reservoirs are miles away from the city. The water comes to the city through great pipes that are under the ground. Smaller pipes take the water to the houses.

Look at the water pipes inside your house. See how the water goes into the rooms of your house.

Water is stored for use on farms. In places where there is little rain, farmers used to have a hard time. Their crops did not grow well. But today fine farms are found where everything used to be so dry.

Water is brought to the fields through great ditches. The water sometimes travels for hundreds of miles through the ditches.

Smaller ditches take water from the big ditch to the different farms. At the farms water runs out of the ditches and over the ground. It waters the ground so that crops can grow.

Food crops can now grow in these dry places because men have learned to store up water.

Where Does the Salt Go?

Most children like to play with water. You can learn something new by playing with water.

Put a little salt into some water. Very soon you cannot see the salt. Where has it gone?

Put a little sugar into some water. By and by you cannot see the sugar. Where has the sugar gone?

Do you know the word *dissolve*? When things dissolve in water, they become a part of the water.

Salt and sugar dissolve in water. You cannot see them in the water. But they are there in the water.

Drink a little of the water in which salt is dissolved. Can you taste the salt? Now drink a little of the water in which sugar is dissolved. Can you taste the sugar?

Put some soap flakes into warm water. Soon the soap goes all through the water. It is dissolved in the water.

At first there are bubbles in the water. Let it stand for a while. Do not stir it. Now most of the bubbles are gone. You can see the soap all through the water. The soap has become part of the water.

Things dissolved in water become a part of the water.

Put a small stone into a glass of water. Stir it around and around. Does the stone become a part of the water?

Find Out by Trying

Try to find out more about dissolving things in water.

Does paper dissolve in water? Does wood? Try to dissolve many small things in water. Which things will dissolve? Which things will not dissolve?

Watch out for this. Some things can be stirred around in water, but they do not dissolve.

Sawdust can be stirred around in water. For a short time you can see it all through the water. You may think that it will be dissolved. But soon you will see the sawdust floating on the top of the water.

Put some sand in water. Stir it around and around. What happens to the sand? Does it float? Does it dissolve?

Put some oil in water. Stir it around. What happens to the oil?

How Long Is a Lifetime?

Lifetime of Animals

Here are Jack and Shep. Shep is an old dog. He has been Jack's dog from the time Jack was a little baby.

Shep has had good care. But he cannot run and play as he used to do. He cannot go swimming with the boys. Someone must always go with Shep now when he takes a walk.

Poor old Shep! He does not see so well as he used to see. Some of his teeth are gone. He cannot eat bones. His food must be soft food.

Many dogs do not live as long as Shep has lived. How old do you think Shep is? He is eleven years old.

Jack is almost as old as Shep. But Jack is not old. Jack feels very young when his mother says to him, "No, you cannot do that. Wait till you are eleven or twelve."

A boy is young when he is eleven years old. But a dog is old when he is eleven. The life of a dog is not nearly so long as the life of a man.

Every spring, many, many hundreds of May flies fly about together. Their eggs are laid in water. The young live in water for about two years. On a spring day they come out of the water and fly away on their new wings.

They fly in the air with other May flies. They fly all through the night, and then their life is over.

An earthworm lives about two years. After it comes out of the egg, it lives and grows through the summer. In winter it stays deep in the ground. In spring it comes up through the ground. It lives on through another year. Then its lifetime is over.

A white cabbage butterfly has a very short lifetime. The cabbage butterfly lays eggs. Young caterpillars come out of the eggs. The caterpillar makes a pupa. A butterfly comes from the pupa. All this happens in five weeks.

Five weeks is a very short lifetime. But some insects do not live so long as that. Most houseflies live for only two or three days. Many fruit flies do not live for even one day. They come out of the eggs. They lay more eggs. Their lifetime is over before the day is done.

Animals may live to be very, very old.

Some of the large kinds of whales have long lives. Some elephants live to be more than one hundred years old. Some parrots live as long as this, too. Pet parrots sometimes have very long lives.

Some turtles have lived to be more than one hundred years old and still are well and strong. Both land turtles and water turtles live for many years.

Some men and women have lived to be more than one hundred years old. But most people do not live to be nearly as old as that.

Something to Think About

Not all insects have such short lives as those you have read about in this story. Some insects live for many years. One kind of grasshopper or locust lives for seventeen years. It is called the seventeen-year locust.

Not all elephants, parrots, or turtles live to be one hundred years old. Most elephants live for twenty or thirty years. Wild parrots live for about twenty or thirty years too. Most turtles do not live a hundred years, but many turtles live to be very old.

How long is a lifetime? Is it a day or twelve years or twenty years? An animal's lifetime may be as short as a housefly's life or it may be as long as a turtle's life. The lifetime of most animals is not nearly so long as that of people.

Lifetime of Plants

Just a year goes by from one of your birthdays to the next. Suppose you had to live all your life in that one year. Suppose you grew from a baby into an old man or woman in just one year. What a short lifetime that would be!

Many kinds of plants have a lifetime that is not more than a year. These kinds of plants are called annuals.

Many of the bright colored flowers of the summer garden come from annuals.

Some vegetables are annuals. Annuals have many seeds. Some of these seeds plant themselves, but many seeds must be planted by people.

Annuals must be planted every year. Seeds are put into the ground in spring. When the hot days of summer come, these plants begin to have flowers. All through the summer the annuals keep the garden very beautiful.

When fall comes, the annuals begin to die. They cannot live through the cold winter weather.

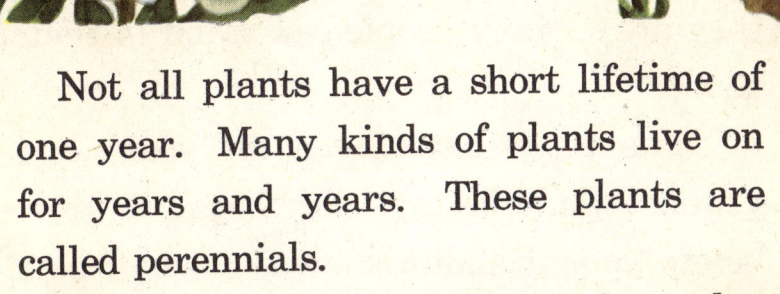

Not all plants have a short lifetime of one year. Many kinds of plants live on for years and years. These plants are called perennials.

Some of our most beautiful garden plants are perennials. Do you know the perennials at the top of this page?

Gardeners and farmers do not like some kinds of perennials. Many kinds of weeds are perennials. Do you know these perennials?

The earth's oldest perennials are trees. Are there some great trees growing near your home? Look up into their branches. How tall these trees are! How strong they are! Many people can stand in their shade.

These trees have lived for years and years. It may be that they began to grow before your grandfather was a small boy.

Can you find a tree that is no taller than yourself? This tree may be much older than you are.

There are trees that have been living for hundreds of years. They were living at the time of the first Christmas. They were old, old trees when the first white men came to this country. Have you ever seen these old, old trees?

Are you thinking of these questions? Why do perennials live for years? Why do they not die as annuals do?

Perennials live a long time because they have food stored away. Most of them have food stored away in their roots. This helps them to live through the long cold winter. It helps them to live through long dry times of year, too.

Annuals do not have food stored away. They have nothing to live on when freezing weather comes, and so they die.

Most perennials live on year after year, but new perennials start each year, too. Perennials have seeds as annuals do. Many of these seeds grow into new plants.

Perennials in Winter

Perennials live through the winter. But they do not grow in this cold time.

How funny it would be if you did not grow in winter! That might make things easier for your mother. You would not grow too big for your clothes so quickly as you do now. But it would take longer for you to grow up.

You grow in winter just as you do in summer because you eat good food all the year round. A perennial cannot make its food in winter. It cannot take water from the soil to help make its food. But a perennial lives on in winter because it has food stored away.

Food is not stored away in your body as it is in a plant. You eat and grow in winter. A perennial lives but it does not grow in winter.

What Plants Need to Grow

The children in Miss Snow's room wanted to have gardens in the windows of their schoolroom.

They took good soil from the outdoor garden and put it into window boxes. Then they started plants in these boxes. They put the plants carefully in the soil.

They worked hard to take care of their plants in the right way. They learned that plants must have the right kind of air. All living things must have air.

They learned that their plants needed warm air. They put their plants where the air was not too dry.

Sometimes a little wind came in through the window or through the door. The children tried to keep wind away from their plants. They tried to give their plants the right kind of air.

Some plants need more water than other plants do. The children had some plants like those in the picture at the top of the page. They put water on these plants every day.

The plants below need little water. The children gave a little water to these plants about once in two weeks.

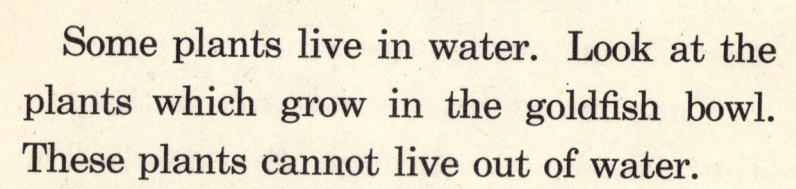

Some plants live in water. Look at the plants which grow in the goldfish bowl. These plants cannot live out of water.

All living things need some water.

The children found out that plants must have light. Some plants need more light than others do, but all of their plants needed some light. The plant in the picture at the top of the page needs much bright sunlight. The children put this plant near the window.

The plant below grows well where the bright sunlight does not reach it.

The children put the plant in a dark room. They watered it every day, but in a short time the plant stopped growing.

Here is the life story of a bean seed.

Do you see the tiny plant in the seed? At first the seed itself gives food to the young plant.

Look at each picture to see how the tiny plant grows and changes. At last it is an old plant. It has seeds of its own.

These seeds go into the ground. The ground is warm and wet. The new plant begins to grow inside the seed. Then the life story takes place all over again.

Why Does It Happen?

Try this on a day in spring.

Dig up some earth from the fields or woods. Soil from your garden will do very well too. Put the earth in a plant jar. Keep the jar of earth in a light place. Water it as you water other plants.

You may have a real surprise. Many kinds of little plants may start to grow.

Some of these plants come from seeds. Some may grow from roots which came up when you were digging.

Try to find out which are annuals and which are perennials.

What makes these plants grow? When you care for them, you help them to have three things which you have been reading about. These three things are light, air, water. Most living things need all three to make them grow.

A Tree Grows Up

A great old maple tree grows in Mary's yard. Its branches are higher than the house. In spring Mary watches the birds as they make nests among the leaves.

She often plays in the shade of the old maple tree. One afternoon more than thirty people sat in its wide shade.

This great tree was once a little seed. The seed had two wings. You have seen many of these seeds. Children sometimes call them " polly noses."

On a bright spring day, the seed left its tree. The warm wind carried it about. It sailed and sailed in the air. It fell to the ground away from the mother tree.

In a few weeks a tiny tree was growing from the seed. This was two hundred years ago. Mary's house was not here at that time. Her grandfather's great-great grandfather was only a boy. There were no railroads in those days. There were no telephones. There were no electric lights. George Washington was a young man.

This tiny tree did not grow up quickly. It did not grow up easily.

At first the ground around its roots was soft and wet. The roots grew and the trunk grew. But then the roots came to hard rock. They could not go straight down into the rock. So they went out around the rock. Under the ground the roots of the big maple tree look like this.

The little tree had to push its way up among many other trees. There were oak trees and other maples. Some of these grew in close around the young maple. They took water from the soil. They made shade so that it was hard for the little tree to get sunlight. But it grew and grew.

Storms came. One night the wind blew down a great tree. It fell against the little tree. It pushed the little tree almost down to the ground.

But the little tree did not stop growing. It was no longer a straight little tree. It grew up around the trunk of the fallen tree.

As the years went by, the young tree grew. It had many seeds of its own. Many birds built nests in its branches.

At last it was a big tree. Then there was fighting in the land. One night the tree saved a man's life. He stayed all night, high up in the wide branches. In the morning he was safe from his enemies.

More and more people came to the land where the tree was growing. They cut down many of the trees. They built houses. A town grew up.

Mary's great-great-grandfather built his house near the tree.

"This is a fine old tree," he said. "We shall take good care of it."

After the other trees were cut down, it was easier for the maple tree to keep on growing. It had more sunlight. There was room in the soil for its roots. It grew bigger and bigger.

Some day a storm may strike down the old maple tree. It may get sick, as a tree sometimes does. Beetles or other insects may try to eat its wood.

But Mary's family will take good care of the tree. They will try to keep away the insects. They will try to keep the tree from getting sick. They want the tree to live on and on.

Mary may be a grandmother some day. Her grandchildren may play in the shade of the old maple tree.

Other Lives

1. People want to help good plants and animals to go on living.

Have you seen men putting something on their trees to keep insects from eating them?

Men take good care of old trees. They work hard to keep them alive. Have you ever seen men filling a hole in an old tree?

242

2. Most towns find some way to give old horses and dogs a good home. How is this done in your town?

3. Mr. White is a very old man. He cannot work as he did at one time. He cannot move about as easily as he did. But he is strong and well. He always has taken good care of himself.

Mr. White tells wonderful stories to boys and girls. He tells them about things that happened when he was a boy. Then their town did not look as it does now. He is a good friend in many ways.

4. What about your own lifetime? What do you do to keep strong and well?

Do you eat the kinds of food that Mother says are good for you? Do you go to bed early?

What else can you do to live and grow through a fine long lifetime?

Index

Air and temperature, 188–193
Air and water, 180–187
Air gliders, 177–179
Air travelers, 174–176
Airplane trip, 168–173
Airport, 168, 169
Animal babies, 34–36, 40–41, 54–55, 61–64, 67–69, 73–74, 104
Animal enemies, 38, 49, 53–54, 65, 95–100
Animal homes, 33–36, 54, 59–61, 67–69, 73–76, 102–133
Animal life and growth, 32–77, 78–101
Animal pet, 77
Animals and their food, 38, 44, 59, 62–64, 70–74, 80–87
Animals and their lifetime, 219–224
Animals in stormy weather, 39–40, 47–48, 56, 66, 88–93
Animals that sleep in winter, 39–40, 92, 93
Animals that taste bad, 49, 99
Animals with hard coverings, 36–38, 98
Annuals, 225–226

Baby cougars, 67–69, 73–74
Baby rabbits, 104
Baby song sparrows, 61–64
Baby sunfish, 54–55, 128
Baby turtles, 34–36, 40–41
Baltimore oriole, 121–122
Bean seeds, 234
Bears, 83, 93
Beavers, 83, 93, 208
Birds and their homes, 59–61, 111–116, 120–125
Birds in winter, 66, 90, 91, 93
Black bears, 83
Body coverings, 88–90, 98
Box turtle, 33–41
Box turtle babies, 34–36, 40–41
Box turtle in winter, 39–40
Box turtle's food, 38
Box turtle's nest, 33–36
Box turtle's shell, 36–38
Butterfly, 42–49, 222
Butterfly and caterpillar, 42–46
Butterfly eggs, 44, 48, 127, 222

Cabbage butterflies, 222
Cat catching mouse, 85
Caterpillar, 42–46, 81, 83, 119, 127, 222
Caterpillar changing to butterfly, 44–46
Cave of cougars, 67–69
Changes of moon, 17–23

245

Chipmunks, 92, 106–108
Clouds, 169–171, 172, 173, 180–181
Coats of animals, 88–90
Cold and heat, 188–193
Color as a protection, 94–95, 125
Cougar homes, 67–69, 73–76
Cougar kittens, 67–69, 73–74
Cougars, 67–76
Cougars catching food, 70–74
Crow's nest, 114

Day, 4–10
Deer, 81, 87, 95
Dissolving things in water, 215–217
Dry cell, 158–163

Eagles, 82, 114, 115, 178
Eagles' nest, 114, 115
Earthworms, 105, 221
Eggs of birds, 61–64, 122–125
Eggs of butterfly, 44, 48, 127, 222
Eggs of fish, 54–55, 128
Eggs of insects, 44, 48, 126–127, 128, 129
Electric bell, 159–162
Electric lights, 146–147
Electric power, 154–157
Electric wires, 156–157, 158
Electricity, 144–167
Electricity and good times, 165–166

Electricity as a danger, 163–164
Electricity carrying messages, 152–153
Electricity helps with work, 148–151
Electricity in the home, 144–145, 154, 156, 157
Electricity on the farm, 150–151
Elephants, 223, 224
Enemies of animals, 38, 49, 53–54, 65, 95–100
Evaporating water, 180–182, 187

Family of cougars, 67–69, 73–74
Family of song sparrows, 59–64
Family of sunfish, 54–55
Father cougar, 67–69, 73–74
Father sunfish, 54, 55
Feathers of birds, 88, 89, 90
Fish, 50–56, 128, 129
Flies, 128, 221, 222
Floods, 211
Flying squirrel, 179
Fog, 169–171, 172–173, 180, 181
Food of animals, 38, 44, 59, 62–64, 70–74, 80–87
Frog catching food, 85
Fruit juices, 204
Fur of animals, 88, 89, 90

Gannets, 116
Gills of fish, 53
Gliders, 177
Grasshopper, 81, 224
Gray squirrels, 90, 112–113, 179

Hawks, 65, 82
Heat and cold, 188–193
Home of box turtle, 33–36
Home of cougars, 67–69, 73–76
Home of song sparrows, 59–61
Home of sunfish, 54
Homes and what they are for, 130–131
Homes and what they are made of, 118–120
Homes built carefully, 121–123
Homes built quickly, 124–125
Homes in high rocky places, 115–117
Homes in trees, 112–114
Homes in water, 109–110, 208
Homes near the ground, 111
Homes of animals, 102–133
Homes on the ground, 104
Homes under the ground, 105–108
Hummingbirds, 123

Insect homes, 105, 119, 126–127, 128, 129, 132

Insects as food, 83, 84

Kittens of cougar, 67–69, 73–74

Larva of butterfly, 44, 45, 127
Larva of mason wasp, 127
Lifetime of animals, 219–224
Lifetime of plants, 225–230
Lions, 81, 84, 86
Locust, 224

Magnet holding things, 134–138, 142
Magnet pulling things, 139–141, 143
Magnets, 134–143
Maple tree, 236–241
Mason wasp, 126–127
May flies, 128, 221
Meat-eating animals, 81
Meat-eating birds, 82
Mice, 83
Monarch butterfly, 42–49
Monarch butterfly and its life, 44–46
Monarch butterfly in summer, 48
Monarch butterfly in winter, 47–48
Moon and conditions on it, 24–29
Moon and its changes, 17–23
Morning, 5–7
Mother cougar, 67–69, 73–74

247

Mother song sparrow, 61–64
Mother sunfish, 54
Mother turtle, 36
Mother wasp, 126, 127
Mountain homes, 115–117
Mountain sheep, 116–117
Mountains on the moon, 25–27
Muskrats, 109–110

Nests made by birds, 59–61, 111–116, 120–125
Nests made by fish, 54, 128
Nests made by insects, 119, 126–127
Nests made by rabbits, 104
Nests made by squirrels, 112–113
Nests made by turtles, 33–36
Night, 11–12
Nighthawk, 124, 125

Oriole, 121–122
Owls, 65, 82

Parrots, 223, 224
Perennials, 227–230
Pet in the out-of-doors, 77
Planes, 169–173, 177
Plants and their lifetime, 225–230
Plants and their needs, 209, 231–235
Plants as food, 80, 81, 83

Protection from cold, 88–93
Protection from enemies, 38, 49, 53–54, 65, 95–100
Protection of trees, 242
Pupa of butterfly, 45–46

Rabbits, 80, 90, 92, 104
Radio, 152, 153
Rain, 210, 211
Rats, 83
Reservoir for water, 194–195, 212–214
Rocks on the moon, 25–27
Rocky places for homes, 115–117
Roots of plants, 209
Roots of trees, 238

Sailing through the air, 177–179
Salmon, 128, 129
Scales of fish, 51
Sea birds, 116, 176
Sea gulls, 176, 178
Seeds as food, 59, 82, 84
Seeds of plants, 234, 235, 237
Seventeen-year locust, 223
Shadows, 6–9
Shadows and sunlight, 13–16
Sheep, 116–117
Sky at night, 11–12
Sky in the daytime, 4–10
Snails, 80
Song sparrow, 57–66
Song sparrow babies, 61–64

Song sparrow enemies, 65
Song sparrows and where they live, 57
Song sparrows in winter, 66
Song sparrows' nest, 59-61
Sparrows, 57-66
Squirrels, 81, 90, 112-113
Steam, 207
Steam engine, 207
Stormy petrel, 176
Sunfish, 50-56
Sunfish and how they breathe, 52-53
Sunfish and how they look, 50-51
Sunfish babies, 54-55
Sunfish enemies, 53-54
Sunfish in winter, 56
Sunfish nest, 54
Sunlight and shadows, 13-16
Sunrise, 5-6
Sunset, 10
Swallows, 120

Telegraph, 153
Telephone, 152, 153
Temperature of the air, 188-192
Temperature of the body, 192, 193
Thermometers and their use, 188-193
Tigers, 81, 86
Traveling in the air, 168-176
Traveling on the water, 206

Tree growing up, 236-241
Trees, 228, 242
Trees as homes, 112-114
Turtles, 33-41, 223, 224

Vegetables, 204

Wasps, 119, 120, 126-127, 132
Water and its uses, 194-217
Water helping things, 206-209
Water hurting things, 210-211
Water in our bodies, 201-203
Water in plants, 204-205
Water in the air, 180-187, 198
Water in the ground, 200
Water on the earth, 199
Water plants, 80
Water tanks, 212-214
Watering the land, 214
Wells of water, 200
Whales, 223
Whippoorwill, 124, 125
Wildcats, 81
Wings and their use, 178
Winter coats of animals, 88-90
Winter homes of animals, 39-40, 47, 56, 66, 91-92, 107-108, 109, 110, 113
Wolves, 87
Woodchucks, 80, 92
Woodpeckers, 113

Yellow jacket wasps, 132
Yellow warblers, 111

Vocabulary List

Science Every Day is the third book of a series entitled OUR WORLD OF SCIENCE. The total vocabulary of the book is 843 words. Of these words, 657 are introduced and taught in the earlier volumes of OUR WORLD OF SCIENCE or are found in a basic reading vocabulary for grades one and two.

Science Every Day also uses 186 new words necessary to the development of science concepts. These new words are gradually introduced. No more than four of them appear on any page, and 95 per cent of the new words are used four times or more. Variant forms are not counted as new words when they are derived by adding *s, es, 's, ed, ing, er, est, ly, y, n,* or *en* to a known word. A compound formed by combining two known words is not counted as a new word; nor is either part of a known compound when used alone.

The list below includes the new words by pages:

5 self	16 . . .	32 . . .	45 fastens
asleep	17 meet	33 . . .	hangs
6 east	18 since	34 leaf	bottom
west	19 Jip	35 touch	pupa
buttoned	20 . . .	those	46 folded
jacket	21 month	spread	47 saves
7 . . .	22 quarter	36 laid	hundreds
8 noon	second	shell	48 . . .
strikes	full	bone	49 bad
twelve	23 third	37 . . .	50 sunfish
9 swing	24 answered	38 enemies	Polly
caps	25 . . .	snails	clear
10 limb	26 . . .	39 wiggled	51 scales
tonight	27 feet	40 . . .	scratched
11 . . .	pointed	41 . . .	52 . . .
12 factories	28 . . .	42 caterpillar	53 gills
stars	29 breathe	milkweed	54 . . .
13 Martha	30 careful	stripes	55 . . .
body	31 . . .	43 taste	56 . . .
14 . . .		monarch	57 . . .
15 wondered		44 life	58 . . .
page		larva	

59 . . .
60 . . .
61 . . .
62 . . .
63 . . .
64 . . .
65 hawks
66 wrens
   warblers
   swallows
67 cougars
68 cave
   among
69 . . .
70 claws
   teeth
71 lies
72 colts
   calves
   miles
73 meat
   themselves
74 . . .
75 branches
76 . . .
77 ants
   grasshoppers
78 cardinal
   beetles
   woodpeckers
79 tunnel
80 grain
   vegetables
81 nuts
   crops
   tigers
82 eagles
   carry
   chickadees
   jays
83 . . .
84 spiders
   wolves
   zebra

85 watchfully
   tongue
86 fighters
   deep
   bite
87 . . .
88 leggings
89 . . .
90 . . .
91 close
   needles
   thick
   cornstalks
92 trunk
   curl
93 muskrats
94 . . .
95 . . .
96 . . .
97 . . .
98 . . .
99 . . .
100 . . .
101 question
102 . . .
103 . . .
104 . . .
105 wasps
106 . . .
107 . . .
108 . . .
109 . . .
110 built
111 . . .
112 . . .
113 . . .
114 . . .
115 . . .
116 gannets
117 . . .
118 . . .

119 . . .
120 . . .
121 Baltimore
122 . . .
123 humming-
    birds
124 whippoorwill
125 . . .
126 mason
127 stings
128 May flies
    salmon
129 . . .
130 . . .
131 . . .
132 . . .
133 . . .
134 . . .
135 . . .
136 twenty
    thirty
    desk
137 pins
    ring
138 steel
139 . . .
140 . . .
141 . . .
142 middle
143 corks
144 . . .
145 . . .
146 electric
147 below
    read
148 . . .
149 Davis
150 send
151 . . .

152 words
    telephone
153 sent
    messages
    telegraph
154 bulbs
155 . . .
156 power
    wires
157 . . .
158 cell
159 posts
160 . . .
161 pathway
162 . . .
163 . . .
164 . . .
165 . . .
166 . . .
167 . . .
168 . . .
169 fog
170 . . .
171 dipped
172 . . .
173 . . .
174 flap
175 gulls
176 petrel
177 kites
    gliders
178 wide
179 skin
180 . . .
181 . . .
182 . . .
183 . . .
184 . . .
185 become
186 . . .
187 . . .

188 thermometer	202 blood	216 soap	230 . . .
shade	203 . . .	217 sawdust	231 . . .
189 . . .	204 juicy	218 lifetime	232 . . .
190 temperature	watermelon	219 Shep	233 . . .
line	205 slice	220 eleven	234 . . .
number	206 . . .	221 . . .	235 . . .
191 degrees	207 . . .	222 . . .	236 maple
192 . . .	208 whales	223 parrots	237 George
193 . . .	209 . . .	224 locust	Washington
194 . . .	210 . . .	seventeen	238 . . .
195 . . .	211 . . .	225 annuals	239 . . .
196 tank	212 reservoirs	226 . . .	240 . . .
197 . . .	213 . . .	227 perennials	241 . . .
198 . . .	214 ditches	228 . . .	242 . . .
199 map	215 salt	229 . . .	243 . . .
200 . . .	sugar		
201 lemonade	dissolve		

PRINTED IN THE UNITED STATES OF AMERICA